"[This] concept is refreshingly simple, yet the book is full of fresh and clever ideas as well as uncomplicated recipes that I will make time and time again. *Pour Together* serves as a reminder that delicious doesn't have to be difficult, and some of our most enduring cocktails—look no further than the Martini, Manhattan, or Whiskey Highball—are classics not in spite of but because of their approachability."
—**NICK FAUCHALD, cookbook author and coauthor of *Death & Co***

"As someone who makes 'complicated' drinks for a living, making myself a drink at home always feels strangely daunting. Roger Kamholz shares my love of a delicious and complex cocktail and, like me, doesn't want to have to pull out a bag of gadgets to make that happen at home. These two-ingredient recipes come together in mere minutes, but the flavor combinations are layered and thoughtful."
—**NATASHA DAVID, author and recipe developer**

POUR
TOGETHER

PHOTOGRAPHS BY SUECH & BECK

PO
TOGE

CLARKSON POTTER/PUBLISHERS NEW YORK

ROGER KAMHOLZ

UR
THER

2-Ingredient Cocktails to Meet Every Mood

Published in the United States by Clarkson Potter/Publishers, an imprint of the Crown Publishing Group, a division of Penguin Random House LLC, New York. ClarksonPotter.com

CLARKSON POTTER is a trademark and POTTER with colophon is a registered trademark of Penguin Random House LLC.

Library of Congress Cataloging-in-Publication Data
Names: Kamholz, Roger, author.
Title: Pour together: 2-ingredient cocktails to meet every mood / Roger Kamholz; photographs by Suech and Beck.
Description: New York: Clarkson Potter/Publishers, [2025] | Includes index.
Identifiers: LCCN 2024017935 (print) | LCCN 2024017936 (ebook) |
ISBN 9780593798751 (hardcover)
ISBN 9780593798768 (ebook)
Subjects: LCSH: Cocktails. | LCGFT: Cookbooks.
Classification: LCC TX951 .K148 2025 (print) | LCC TX951 (ebook) | DDC 641.87/4--dc23/eng/20240517
LC record available at https://lccn.loc.gov/2024017935
LC ebook record available at https://lccn.loc.gov/2024017936

ISBN 978-0-593-79875-1
Ebook ISBN 978-0-593-79876-8

Printed in China

Editor: Darian Keels
Art Director: Stephanie Huntwork
Designer: Stephanie Huntwork
Contributing designer: Yasmeen Bandoo
Production editor: Liana Faughnan
Production manager: Jessica Heim
Compositors: Merri Ann Morrell and Hannah Hunt
Food stylist: Melanie Stuparyk
Prop stylist: Andrea McCrindle
Copy editor: Anne Cherry
Proofreaders: Eldes Tran and Andrea Peabbles
Indexer: Elizabeth Parson
Publicist: Natalie Yera-Campbell
Marketer: Allison Renzulli

10 9 8 7 6 5 4 3 2 1

First Edition

To my dad, Steve.

CON[T]

ENTS

Introduction

For the better part of two decades, cocktails have fascinated me. I read about them. I report on their goings-on. I fray the patience of bartenders with endless questions about them. I've attempted to master making my own concoctions. And boy, do I find great pleasure in drinking them. When it comes to cocktails, I am a student, a scribe, a tinkerer, and, if I'm being honest, sort of a groupie.

Until now, in sitting down to ink a whole book on cocktails, I hadn't dwelled much on *why* I fell so hard (figuratively) for this one particular domain of beverage culture. So, I thought for a while about what fuels this unshakable crush of mine.

The story of cocktails appeals to the journalist in me. I spent many of my young-writer years living in Chicago as witness and customer to the amazing rise of the city's modern cocktails and spirits culture. I started to document the scene for local publications like *The Chicagoist* and later, Serious Eats. (Venues for cocktail journalism grew over this period as well, including the addition of PUNCH, where I contribute presently.) Meanwhile, seminal books like David Wondrich's *Imbibe!* came along to complement my barstool education. What I learned is that mixed drinks have a long, colorful past, decorated with gumptious characters and embellishments to sort through. We're lucky to be still living through the best of times, when the drinks and the community of talented people making them are at their finest. Bartending was, before Prohibition, a much-admired profession; great bartenders were treated like celebrities. Prohibition disrupted that trajectory for decades, but today the craft is reinvigorated and as alive as ever. There's so much to say and celebrate about cocktail culture. As you flip through this book, I hope noise from this centuries-old party is audible.

Making drinks is also a creative, culinary discipline, and the sandbox is as big as the world. The supply of ingredients with which to experiment is ever-growing. Distillates have been the traditional anchor of a cocktail, but today really anything potable is in play. And there are equally great drinks to be made across the range of alcohol content, starting from none at all in a zero-proof cocktail, to the stiffest tiki drink concocted with a slew of different rums.

Tastiness is another lure, of course. When the essential mechanics of a cocktail—flavor, aroma, texture, balance, and presentation—roll up into a delicious, cohesive package, I'm content, appreciative.

But what I came to recognize is that none of the above reasons fully explains my obsession. Yes, a well-made drink communicates in a physical, material way that delivers units of worldly pleasure. But that's not unique; many foods do the same. Cocktails hold more meaning.

So I dug deeper. I backtracked through past encounters I've been fortunate to have with truly exceptional cocktails. All those essential elements I mentioned a moment ago were in harmony. The drinks possessed personality and complexity. My palate was happy. But the cocktails I remember best also had a quality that was suprasensory.

Each one grabbed my full attention with a single sip. Each was posture-altering. Delight washed over me in the experience of a transformation: in the glass was stuff that occupied a state of being belonging to none of its raw materials. A Dry Martini once had this effect on me. I had had many before, but I count this one as my first. Bracing, bright, and alive as spring, this Martini unmasked all those others that came before it as imposters. Familiarity with the work of gin and vermouth on their own doesn't prepare you for the music of an unforgettable Martini. That—chasing the moment gold springs from lesser metals—is what's kept me pulled up close to cocktails all this time.

To come back briefly to history, it's worth pointing out that the old practice of alchemy, of attempting to turn lead into gold, isn't so distant a relative from that of mixing drinks. The word *alchemy* comes to us bearing the patina of Arabic, but its origins are ancient. Some scholars see its roots in a Greek term, *kymia,* which means **"pour together."**

The connection to mixing makes sense: the alchemist's chief project was to invent *elixir*—a liquid that could manifest precious metal, but also prolong life. Today we accept that no such thing as elixir exists; nothing can do all that. And yet, when a cocktail takes the edge off a day, or inaugurates a meal, or brings friends together for a celebration, who's to say that drink hasn't helped put a bit more life in our pockets?

Truly exceptional cocktails, I came to realize, perform magic tricks. They can turn out different, better, and more interesting than the individual things that made them. Truly exceptional cocktails, like well-selected vinyls to accompany a late-night dinner party, can give our mood a new rhythm. They color in the beauty of an occasion.

Throughout their history, the majority of mixed drinks contain four, five, or even more ingredients. As you read this, the best cocktail bars around the world are busy devising new ones. I love that for them. Keep it up! Make those beautiful and intricately layered drinks, like houses of cards stacked high. I adore those drinks for being well-thought-out treatises on flavor and texture and balance. Yet I am also here to tell you, with the long-windedness of a whole book, that leaning one card against another—as modest in ambition as that may sound—can work magic, as well. In fact, I would argue there's no more remarkable alchemy in the realm of cocktails than when but a pair of ingredients pour together to make magic happen.

That's why we're here, and what the journey we're about to embark on is about. Because I'll confess, as much as I love enjoying elaborate cocktails at bars, at home I often favor simpler preparations. The results you can achieve with two ingredients are bigger, broader, and more delicious than you probably expect. That riveting Dry Martini, along with many other drinks, is proof of that.

You may have arrived here because you are living on your own for the first time and are trying your hand at entertaining. Or you are looking for easy yet elevated drinks you can bring to picnics in the park that aren't just beer or wine. Maybe you're tired of only mixing one-note Screwdrivers. Or maybe there's a special person in your life, and how great would it be to send them a love letter in a glass? The drink that becomes their usual because you make it, and you make it best. There are countless reasons for a tidy, tasty, two-ingredient cocktail, and I'm here for you, to make all those moments, big and small, more delicious and special.

The experienced cocktail maker, too, can find value here. Treat this book like an invitation to explore a way of bartending at home where the ingredients are allowed to shine. You will find some classic cocktails you've perhaps never tried before, and new originals that get your own creative juices flowing. Many of the drinks in this book follow a template—spirit plus vermouth, for example, the basis for the Martini. You can take that template and go in so many directions, and I have given lots of prompts on how to adapt and enhance drinks with add-ons and modifications.

This book gives guidance on setting up a home bar, selecting from the dizzying array of products available, and building up a repertoire of cocktails you can make on the spot—a handy bit of proficiency when, say, you want to unwind on a weeknight or friends pop over for an impromptu dinner. The recipes collected here are easy to learn and remember, by design.

My goal for you is to get comfortable with the techniques, while at the same time introducing you to the wide variety and unprecedented quality of liquid resources available to today's home bartenders. Beer and wine will make appearances. We'll play a little loose with the rules.

Some cocktails are straightforward, where the ingredients are available at stores and ready to pour right out of their vessel and into yours. If meal prep for you means delivery apps and making reservations, don't worry: the culinary techniques involved in creating cocktail ingredients are easy to learn and execute. Owing to their harmonizing powers, the drinks in this book are grouped by the moods and occasions they suit. For example, wishing for something breezy like a Sunday afternoon? Try a Bright Sip (pages 28–47). Need to tie off a tough day? Enlist a Weeknightcap (pages 48–67). To upgrade a sunlit afternoon into a full-blown holiday, reach for snackable, sessionable cocktails that make up the section called Drinking & Nibbling (pages 68–83).

As a student of cocktails for the past twenty years, cocktail bars have been my classroom. When I'm sitting across from a glinting back bar stocked with bottles, I naturally peruse the labels, looking for ones I don't recognize. I read drink menus the same way. Words I don't know spark a conversation, an opportunity to learn (and sample) something new. This adventure has led me to meet and befriend passionate and creative people. It's given me inspiration to write. It colors the way I travel. My takeaway has been, there's excitement and opportunity in the unfamiliar. I encourage you to seek out the drink you least expect to like. You can't appreciate a duet only by considering its ingredients alone.

Before We Pour

WHAT COUNTS AS A TWO-INGREDIENT COCKTAIL? (DOES SUCH A THING EXIST?)

The general idea of a two-ingredient cocktail carries with it some conundrums. To appreciate why, we must travel back to the cocktail's conceptual birthplace: the pages of a regional newspaper in New York's Hudson Valley.

On May 13, 1806, *The Balance, and Columbian Repository* published the first known description of what a cocktail is, giving us its component parts: "a stimulating liquor, composed of spirits of any kind, sugar, water and bitters." This day is now celebrated as World Cocktail Day.

At the time when they arose to become a thing unto themselves, cocktails stood apart from juleps, crustas, cups, punches, and the numerous other then-popular categories of sippables. What we today call the Old-Fashioned—whiskey, sugar or simple syrup, (usually) orange peel, and bitters, diluted with ice—is probably the most exemplary expression of this traditional template. Originally this concoction was likely just known as a whiskey cocktail. The drink (much like many other basic cocktails) spawned various riffs during the mixed-drink-mad 1800s, to the degree that late-nineteenth-century bargoers had to start specifying the old-fashioned whiskey cocktail—then later just "the Old-Fashioned"—when they wanted to dispense with all the fuss and just get the original. We didn't have to call them acoustic guitars until electric came along.

Going off the 1806 definition, a true cocktail would appear to be, at the very least, a trio of elements uniting. Ergo, the notion of a two-ingredient cocktail . . . well, it doesn't snuggle up all cozy-cozy with this historical meaning. But our vernacular has a way of modifying over time, and the word *cocktail* has since been widely adopted as shorthand for mixed drinks at large, with and without alcohol. In the world between these book covers, we embrace this fuzzier, more inclusive conception of what a cocktail can be. Simply put, a two-ingredient cocktail is and it isn't—it exists but also doesn't—and that's okay. Notwithstanding this uncertainty, you can expect to find some very Cocktail-esque cocktails in here—that is, drinks composed of two ingredients that together reach a "stimulating," spirit-forward, and bittersweet result, reminiscent of drinks like the Old-Fashioned that launched the craze for cocktails. When a cocktail in the book harkens back to the classic 1806 template, we'll point that out. And when it doesn't, I ask you to join me in embracing the magic that happens when we allow two ingredients to shine.

With that neatly out of the way, let's move on to another philosophical question: What constitutes a two-ingredient cocktail? (Emphasis on the two-ness.) Multiple things might be involved in bringing a mixed drink to fruition, but not all that stuff qualifies as ingredients. For our purposes, a two-ingredient cocktail marries a pair of primary contributors of flavor, and the interplay of those two elements makes up the soul of the drink. Think of it this way: a two-ingredient cocktail might have a small supporting cast, but it is only ever going to have two co-stars.

Take water, for example. Water plays a role in most cocktails. In fact, its job is very important. Water in its solid state (aka ice) keeps a drink pleasantly cold and, by melting, moderates the intensity of the taste of alcohol through dilution. Water when acting as a CO_2-saturated solution (aliases include seltzer, club soda, mineral water) can do wonders to the way a cocktail washes over the palate. But water is predominantly neutral in flavor on its own. We use it to lengthen, froth, chill, and, occasionally, heat up our drinks. It's no more an *ingredient* in a cocktail than the whisk that emulsifies a vinaigrette or the oven that roasts a turkey. Again, this is in no way meant to diminish what water means to a cocktail. The purity of the water we use in our cocktails is crucial, as is the caliber of the ice. Wet, jagged, sloppy, gas-station bagged ice wrecks a cocktail, prompting it to go bland too fast. (This stuff is wholly undeserving of the nickname "party ice.") Making nice ice—hard, dry on its surface—for your mixed drinks isn't difficult or costly, and it can be a game-changing upgrade. (We'll return to the subject of ice shortly.) Moreover, the style, freshness, and grit of the ebullience of carbonated water matter greatly. That half-finished, loosely capped 1-liter seltzer in the back of the fridge from who knows when? It's going to render your cocktail as lifeless and unappealing as mushy leftovers. Unopened or newly charged seltzer is a must.

In short, we are going to treat water like a tool that happens to be potable rather than as an ingredient. Some might see this as a controversial stance. I am okay with that, too. Have water handy in all its various forms, as many of us generally do already.

What about garnishes? The job of a garnish is to bring visual and aromatic enhancement to a cocktail, but we're not going to count a cocktail's garnish as a full-blown ingredient here, either. At most, garnishes are ingredient-*ish*. They tend to reside on the fringes of drinks. Consuming them is optional. Throughout these pages, you'll find that adding them is also optional—it's your cocktail! Consider one of the most garnish-influenced cocktails, the Gibson (page 118): it's a Martini variant consisting of gin and dry vermouth served with a pickled pearl onion. Subtract the onion, and you'd no longer have a Gibson. And yet, you can certainly enjoy a Gibson without consuming the onion. The same cannot be said for the gin and the vermouth. That's my logic and I'm sticking to it.

This book is stocked with recipes that rely only on "off-the-shelf" ingredients—meaning bottles that you can purchase and use as is. This is intentional, so that making drinks from this book is approachable and easy for the readers who are newer to mixing. Making excellent drinks need not be complicated. That said, I've also included recipes that ask for an ingredient to be homemade. That ingredient is going to require ingredients of its own to make. This is part of the fun of making your own drinks and a way to develop your skills. It's more work, but you'll feel more ownership over the finished product.

A PRIMER ON TOOLS, TECHNIQUES & GLASSWARE

Like most hobbies, homemade cocktailing has an abundant gear culture. Those who are so inclined can load up on truly exquisite bar tools, glassware, and advanced ice-molding technologies, all the while parting with tidy sums of cash. I'm not going to argue against a handsome bar setup; in a lot of cases, these materials add value and pleasure to the whole theater of preparing and imbibing cocktails. But what I've always appreciated about cocktail making as a hobby is that you can get going in it with not much stuff, and for not much money.

TOOLS

With a few exceptions, the drinks in this book don't require a lot of tools to prepare. Moreover, many kitchen tools you may already own can double as bar tools. The following items are some to consider investing in to get your home bar in working order.

ICE CUBE TRAYS
Look for straight-sided silicone trays, whose flexibility makes it easy to pop the cubes out. Sizes and shapes vary. I like the trays that freeze one-inch cubes, which are great for shaking, stirring, and serving cocktails. Explore spherical molds and mini-cube trays to enhance the presentation of your drinks.

"KITCHEN DRAWER" MULTITASKERS
Again, many of the items you are already probably cooking with can moonlight at the home bar. Things like a cutting board, paring knife, citrus press or other juicing tool, fine-mesh strainer, whisk, food-grade spray bottle (aka an atomizer), vegetable peeler—these don't really need to be cocktail specific, per se. Y-shaped peelers give you wide citrus peels with consistent thickness, so I prefer those. A well-stocked kitchen drawer will have you cocktailing in no time.

SPECIALIZED COCKTAIL TOOLS

This equipment isn't as cross-functional as the kitchen drawer multitaskers, but the tools are purpose built for essential techniques and thus easily prove their worth after a couple of uses.

- **A long, weighted barspoon** with a spiral neck gives you optimal control when you're stirring drinks. The narrow scoop is useful for fishing a cocktail cherry or onion out of a jar. (Some barspoons have fork ends that are even better for this purpose.) The spiral neck is useful in pouring seltzer, sparkling wine, and other carbonated elements into a drink glass in a way that preserves their bubbles.

- **Shaker tins, mixing glasses, and their complementary strainers** enable you to execute the most-used moves in bartending: shaking and stirring. I prefer to use shaker tins that fit together—or a pint glass paired with a single large shaker tin—over the so-called cobbler shaker, which has a lid with built-in strainer, as these tend to leak. There are a few types of strainers. The julep strainer looks like a round spoon with biggish holes and is used for straining stirred drinks built in a mixing glass. A hawthorne strainer is flat-topped, slotted, and ringed with a spring so it can fit snugly into the mouth of a shaker tin, pint glass, or a mixing glass. The design catches ice chips and other solids, so it is ideal for straining shaken drinks. I primarily use my hawthorne strainer, because it can strain stirred drinks as effectively as the julep strainer does. However, if you want to pursue throwing—a resurgent technique that involves passing a cocktail's liquid contents between shaker tins in ribbony, exaggerated pours—then a julep is the better choice of strainer because it enables you to cage ice in one strainer while allowing the liquid to easily pass back and forth.

- **For measuring out volumes of liquids, jiggers** are the popular go-to. These tools usually have two opposing cups that normally are sized in 2:1 ratios (for instance, 1 ounce and ½ ounce). Despite their popularity, I don't much care for these tools and prefer a 4-ounce spouted measuring cup. Most jiggers are designed to be filled to the brim to reach the correct amount, risking accidental spills. That's less likely to happen with the measuring cup. You can also more easily double up recipes, to yield two drinks in fewer pours with the 4-ounce cup. Plus, the mini measuring cup can pull double duty in the bar and the kitchen.

- **Accessories and extras.** As drinks you make get tastier, the next frontier is to dress them up. Metal straws for highballs are classy and reusable, and metal skewers bring an elevated touch to garnishes like olives, cherries, and rolled citrus twists—quite literally, because you can perch them on the rim of your drink glass.

TECHNIQUES

There are several ways to construct a cocktail. The ideal technique for a drink depends on what degree of help the elements will need to marry together, and how much dilution must be introduced to make it pleasing to the palate. Spirits-only drinks generally call for stirring with ice in a mixing glass, as those ingredients don't need much coaxing to integrate with each other. The chilling and dilution happen gradually when stirring. You may need to stir a drink for a minute to reach a desirable temperature. Cocktails with juices are usually shaken with ice, as this helps to incorporate the heavier solids in juice throughout, leading to a more uniform consistency. Shaking introduces aeration, which makes for a creamy texture and cloudy appearance. Shaking chills and dilutes a beverage much faster than stirring does; in as little as 10 or so seconds you can achieve the same effect as a prolonged stir.

STIRRING

You'll need a mixing glass, julep or hawthorne strainer, and barspoon. It takes a little practice to acquire your dexterity with a barspoon, so begin to train yourself using ice and water. Slide the spoon down to the bottom of your mixing glass, scoop facing in, hugging the inside wall. Grip the barspoon roughly at its midpoint like you would a chopstick, then trace the circumference of the glass while allowing the spoon to rotate between your fingers. The goal is to get all the contents flowing with equal momentum in a whirlpool motion. There should be little to no sound of clacking ice.

SHAKING

By contrast, when you shake a cocktail, clacking the ice is encouraged. You'll need a large and small shaker tin (or a large tin and a pint glass), a hawthorne strainer, and a fine-mesh handheld strainer. After assembling the drink components and ice in the large tin, slide on the companion tin or pint glass to form a seal, and "lock" together with a firm knock on the bottom of the downward-facing piece. I like to hold the assembly sideways in both hands as I shake it in sharp, vigorous motions back and forth, coupled with a slight clockwise rotation. Picture the path described by the pistons on a locomotive. You know you're chilling the contents well when frost appears on the exterior of the tin(s). To separate, point the large tin down and nudge the assembly at the spot where the pieces conjoin in a straight line. This should "unlock" them, allowing you to pull the upper piece (the small tin or pint glass) up and off. Hold it over the large tin for a beat to allow the last few drops to drip down. To strain the liquid, grab your hawthorne strainer and handheld strainer. Fit on the hawthorne and float the strainer in between the tin and the drinking glass to catch small solids. The aforementioned process is the standard method of shaking. There are variant techniques that perform certain specialized tasks. A so-called dry shake is done with liquid ingredients and no ice, commonly when a drink includes egg white or aquafaba, a vegan alternative, and the goal is to whip up foam. If you include a swath of citrus peel in the shaker, that's called a regal shake. Occasionally a recipe will instruct you to forgo straining and pour the shaker contents right into a glass, referred to as a dirty dump.

PRE-CHILLING

If you go to the trouble of stirring and shaking your drinks down to an arctic temperature, don't then pour them into room temperature glassware. Before you use them, chill serving glasses in the fridge or freezer, or fill them with ice water for at least a few minutes. The same goes for your mixing glass.

GLASSWARE

This is a corner of cocktailing where you can showcase your personal aesthetic. Mine is a mismatched collection, built over the years with thrifted antiques and pickups from travels. Sizes, shapes, and designs abound, with different formats suited for different styles of cocktail. But you don't necessarily need to procure each unique type of drink glass out there. Firstly, be mindful of the styles of drinks you prefer and lean more heavily into glassware recommended for those styles. Secondly, so long as you are stocked with examples representing a few broad categories, outlined below, your bases will be covered.

TALL AND SLENDER

This category suits highballs and Collins drinks, which often include carbonation and are served over ice. The capacity of these glasses can range from around 8 ounces up to 14 ounces. The narrowness of the glass helps to slow the dispersal of carbonation, so your bubbly drink stays that way longer. Collins glasses tend to be taller, more slender, and larger in capacity than highball glasses. These are distinct from the pint glass, a 16-ouncer that tends to have a mouth wider than its base and is generally used to serve beer.

STEMMED

Coupes, cocktail glasses, Martini glasses, champagne glasses, Nick and Nora glasses—there's a long list of styles of glass that fall into this category. These are going to hold drinks that are served "up"—without ice in the glass. The capacity of stemmed glasses can vary a lot, although the cocktails that go in them skew smaller in volume, 3 to 5 or so ounces.

LOW AND WIDE

The vessels in this grouping go by many names: tumblers, Old-Fashioned glasses, double Old-Fashioned glasses, rocks glasses, and lowball glasses. The mouth diameter of these glasses tends to be roughly in line with their height, giving them profiles that are squarish in proportion. Noncarbonated cocktails served on ice typically go into one of these squat numbers.

COCKTAIL INGREDIENTS
& THEIR ROLES

Why has the Old-Fashioned remained relevant for centuries? Like many other timeless classic cocktails, its software is just proven to work, so it never became obsolete. The vanilla spice of the whiskey gets a signal boost from the sugar. The sugar's raw sweetness is offset by the bitters. The bitters and the ethanol in the whiskey are tempered by the water. The elements all play a role, and work hand in hand, achieving the Old-Fashioned's equilibrium.

Each drink's architecture is unique, and so is the effect that drink is trying to achieve. For example, just because a drink may lack a sweet or acidic element, that doesn't mean necessarily it's off-balance or incomplete. Its neutral, dry profile might allow that drink's subtler flavors to become the focus. This is important to bear in mind in the arena of two-ingredient cocktails, because we are choosing to be sparing in pulling levers. As such, we select ingredients purposefully, and try to get as much out of them as we can. I'll go into detail about ingredients when they come up in recipes. For now, here's a quick rundown of what to expect.

SPIRITS

Spirits are the backbone of many cocktails. This is the broad category, sometimes called liquor, that includes gin, whiskey, tequila, vodka, brandy, and rum. The fermented "juice" in spirits has gone through distillation, which concentrates its alcohol content. Products within the spirits category can be distinguished in many ways, such as by where their fermentable sugars came from (agave, sugarcane, grain, fruit, etc.); by whether the distillate is aged or unaged; and by what was done to augment the product's flavor—for example, the herbal infusion that gives gin its signature botanical qualities. Owing to their elevated ABV (alcohol by volume; generally, 30 to 40 percent and above), spirits give cocktails aroma, viscosity, and bite.

LIQUEURS

Liqueurs contain distilled alcohol but are lower in ABV than spirits (typically 20 to 30 percent). And, unlike spirits, liqueurs tend to be sweetened. Many liqueurs offer a dominant flavor, such as coffee, cherry, orange, ginger, pear, elderflower . . . the list is voluminous. Most amari fall into the liqueur category. If we think about cocktail ingredients as building blocks, liqueurs are like a split unit—half spirit, half sweet.

WINE, SAKE, AND BEER

These beverages are fermented only (no distillation), so their alcohol content is low (roughly 15 percent and below). Within the wide world of wine, you have sherry and styles of aperitif like vermouth. Born of humble grains of rice, sake can bring a host of delicate flavors to cocktails. And beer remains an undersung choice of cocktail ingredient, particularly today when so many excellent varieties exist. These ingredients are going to lower a cocktail's potency while also adding flavor, adjusting body, and, in some cases, introducing carbonation.

JUICES, SYRUPS, CORDIALS, SHRUBS, SODAS, AND OTHER SO-CALLED MIXERS

These ingredients are typically nonalcoholic, so their main role is to complement and counter the other flavors in a cocktail. With their highly concentrated flavors, bitters are commonly thought of as the seasonings of the bartender's toolkit. A little goes a long way. On the next pages, you'll find two recipes often referenced throughout the text to add to your cocktails and to use up your extra citrus.

Dehydrated Citrus Wheels

In the ratio of effort to effect, serving your cocktails garnished with Dehydrated Citrus Wheels is a clear winner: they're easy to make at home, and will uplevel the presentation of your drinks considerably. Essentially, you're going to use your oven like a food dehydrator. By setting the temperature very low and cooking the wheels for an extended amount of time, their moisture will gently cook off but the solids won't burn.

**YIELDS ABOUT
12 TO 15 PIECES**

3 limes (or other citrus fruits; see Note)

Preheat your oven to its lowest temperature setting, usually 200°F. Choose the oven's convection setting if that's available. Thinly slice wheels from the center third of the fruit, about ⅛ inch thick. Space out the wheels flat on a parchment paper–lined baking sheet. Bake in the oven, flipping the wheels over every 30 minutes to an hour, until they are fully dried out but not burnt. The total cooking time may vary, taking up to 4 to 6 hours. Store in an airtight container for up to 6 months.

NOTE
- For other types of citrus, follow the same process. If you dehydrate a mixed batch, keep in mind that larger, juicier fruits (such as oranges and grapefruits) will take longer to fully dehydrate.

Clarified Lime Juice

Clarified Lime Juice has had the solid bits of pulp that are naturally suspended in fresh lime juice separated out, leaving the liquid-only juice appearing transparent rather than cloudy. It's the key to an exquisitely clear Gin Rickey (page 30). In fact, for any drinks that call for both lime juice and a carbonated mixer (like seltzer), it's beneficial to opt for Clarified Lime Juice because the absence of citrus pulp helps keep the drink from going flat too quickly. Hat tip to cocktail scientist Dave Arnold, who pioneered the technique described here; this recipe follows his experiments in juice clarification.

YIELDS ABOUT 12 OUNCES

100 grams (3½ ounces) water

1 gram agar powder (about ¼ teaspoon)

400 grams (14 ounces) fresh lime juice, room temperature

SPECIAL EQUIPMENT
Cheesecloth

If possible, measure out all the ingredients by weight. Otherwise, use the volumes given. Nest a thin-walled mixing bowl in an ice bath and set aside. Bring the water to a boil in a saucepan over high heat and then add in the agar powder. Lower the heat and simmer the mixture for 2 minutes while lightly whisking. Remove the pan from the heat. Gradually add in the lime juice while whisking the mixture. Pour the saucepan's contents into the mixing bowl. The liquid will start to congeal. Store the mixing bowl, on ice, in the refrigerator for at least 15 minutes to fully set the gel. Remove from the fridge and, using your whisk, break the gel into clumps. Position a cheesecloth-lined strainer over a clean bowl. Transfer the clumps to the cheesecloth. Let the liquid drain through. Gather up the cheesecloth and gently squeeze to maximize the yield. Decant the clarified juice in a resealable bottle and keep refrigerated for up to 1 month.

OCCASIONS, MOODS & HOW TO DRINK THEM: A GUIDE TO USING THIS BOOK

Cocktails have personalities. And when you drink them, a bit of that personality rubs off. A cocktail might make you feel fancy, or mature, or blissfully unplugged. They can become associated with times of day, times in life, places we have been or wish to go, and memories. You can set a mood with a cocktail, or it can be the thing that satisfyingly mirrors the mood you're in.

In this book, I have organized the cocktails into categories based on the moods and occasions they either help bring about or complement. These are not rules delineating why and when to have a particular drink but rather encouragements, sources of inspiration, and if-you-like-that-why-not-try-these invitations. Many recipe pages feature helpful notes as well as "enhancements and departures" meant to empower you to substitute, augment, and experiment with ingredients to discover your signature take on a cocktail. Here's a preview of what each recipe grouping is about.

BRIGHT SIPS

These crispy, low-density drinks are full of aroma and immediacy. Pair with a porch, a picnic, or a Sunday puzzle. They range from dry and botanical to fresh and fruity. Here you'll also find some familiar classics, revamped with new spins, as well as a few historical cocktails that deserve more attention. Many are subtle in alcohol content, so you can indulge in these cocktails without worrying so much about exceeding your limit.

WEEKNIGHTCAPS

On the occasions when, *oy, it was a day,* the most expedient way to declaw it is with a dark-spirited yet bubbly refresher that's ready in no time. Here the shorthand for this style of beverage is Weeknightcap. These carbonated long drinks can stand up to ice, making them right at home perched on the arm of your couch as you unwind awhile.

DRINKING & NIBBLING

Aperitivo hour is that relaxed nonmeal between lunch and dinner where you eat (and drink) lightly to get hungry. Pour the drinks in this group with friends and enjoy with snacks as you watch the sunlight glow orange and imagine yourself in a place with better architecture.

CELEBRATION LIBATIONS

In the mood for a party? Whether you're throwing a wedding, a backyard barbecue—or a backyard wedding for that matter—the right cocktail(s) can dial in the vibe of the occasion. For the formal attire of the cocktail canon, perhaps reach for a Champagne-based number; if shiny were a taste, then these drinks would embody it. Cool and casual events, especially those taking place outdoors, call for easy pours that relax and refresh (*and to which guests can please help themselves,* mumbled busy hosts everywhere). You're in luck, because cultures all over the world have been cracking that case for centuries.

SLOW JAMS

Imagine a weighted blanket, but kind of sexy. Tuck into these spirited sippers and statement drinks when a more full-bodied cocktail is called for. With greater alcohol content, Slow Jams are meant to be enjoyed little by little. Many do the trick of decompressing your digestion after a large meal, and quieting the mind.

SOME ASSEMBLY REQUIRED

Becoming a more experienced drink maker over my adult years has coincided with my self-education in cooking, and the former discipline has naturally borrowed a lot from the latter. Today the kitchen and the bar occupy the same space for me, in my home and in my head. What I've come to know is that with a little culinary know-how, you can expand your cocktail repertoire considerably. If you've come this far, I think you'll be ready to ditch the training wheels. Tackle these project drinks when you're in the mood to make ingredients from scratch. Brunch hosts, bring a homemade touch to your cocktail offering with these. Choose from a range of outspoken flavors, from nutty to woodsy, and hot-and-sour to menthol cool.

BRIGH

Too often we misunderstand lightness as a lack of depth. This confusion has infiltrated our vocabulary, where lightness is a descriptor attached to dull and forgettable stuff. We eat *light bites* rather than a main course; radios play *light FM* when you really want to listen to rock. Lightness in these cases may as well be the silence you hear between heartbeats.

The late, great twentieth-century writer Italo Calvino thought differently. Calvino praised lightness as the embodiment of ingenuity, economy, and agility. Lightness is synonymous with liveliness. It's the quality that enables us to stride over what he called "the weight, the inertia, the opacity of the world" with the swagger of Perseus, skywalking in his winged sandals.

When we think about lightness in a cocktail, I say we follow Calvino's footsteps. A light and bright cocktail ought to be far from toothless and boring, because that's not what lightness is. It can be low in alcohol, or not—to me that's beside the point. More important is the way it transits across the palate: with great presence but leaving little trace.

T SIPS

Among this collection of Bright Sips is a nod to the Gin Rickey—a tall, tart, nineteenth-century drink that contemporary admirers call "air conditioning in a glass." The chills get deeper with the underappreciated Absinthe Frappé, softened with a touch of coconut, as well as the Sgroppino, an Italian creation made with lemon sorbet. Also gifted from Italy, you'll find the glassful of summery sunshine that is the Bellini. We'll bask in the glow of easy-drinking tonics from France and mildly spirited shochu from Japan.

Turn to these Bright Sips to uplift the atmosphere of a dull afternoon, or spring you from the lethargy of a too-hot day. Ingredients range from brisk, botanical spirits to sparkling, floral wines to zesty sodas. Some Bright Sips seek to flirt with our noses as much as our palates. Some are soothing in their clean, dry finish. Others release transfixing flurries of bubbles reminiscent of—if I can borrow a line from the Italian poet Cavalcanti, as translated by Calvino—*white snow falling without wind.*

Each drink has something unique to say, but all speak in the language of lightness.

Gin Rickey

LONDON DRY GIN & LIME JUICE

Washington, DC, isn't known to agree on much, so it says a lot that the capital district has embraced the bubbly and refreshing Gin Rickey as its official drink. This cocktail emerged there in the late 1800s as a riff on the earliest known Rickey, a drink whose creation is credited to (and named after) a lobbyist and saloon owner known as Colonel Joe Rickey. Joe's original Rickey was made with whiskey, not gin; and supposedly he was none too pleased that the Gin Rickey eclipsed his preferred version in renown.

With no sweetener present, the Gin Rickey is all about delivering clean, cold refreshment. (July in DC has been deemed Rickey Month in recognition of the drink's freonic powers.) Serve it tall, in a highball glass to concentrate and slow the release of the seltzer's bubbles, so you experience more of its effervescence for longer. The main stage here is the interaction between your chosen gin and the fresh lime. London dry–style gins tend to be more favorable than modern-day citrus-forward options because they provide a firm juniper counterpoint to the lime juice, but feel free to experiment. I like to use peppery gins like Suncliffe, out of Arizona, and the Dry Rye Gin by California's St. George Spirits.

SERVES 1

2 ounces gin
½ ounce freshly squeezed lime juice

GARNISH

Lime wheel
(see page 24 to use up your extra citrus)

HAVE HANDY

Cubed ice
Seltzer

Add the gin and lime juice to a chilled highball glass. Stir briefly with a barspoon to combine. Stand the barspoon in the glass and pour 5 ounces of seltzer down the neck, filling the glass three-quarters to the top. Gently add in ice to fill. Briefly stir again. Tuck in a lime wheel.

ENHANCEMENTS & DEPARTURES

- Substitute Clarified Lime Juice (page 25) in place of the freshly squeezed lime juice for a cocktail that is crystal clear in appearance and retains its carbonation as you sip.

- Add a small measure of simple syrup to give your Gin Rickey a touch of sweetness. For the syrup: into a small saucepan, add 1 cup of water and 1 cup of granulated sugar, and place over medium-low heat, stirring occasionally. Once the sugar has dissolved, transfer into a resealable container. Use within 2 weeks.

Oolong Hai

OOLONG TEA & SHOCHU

Japan celebrates the highball like nowhere else. The drink format often consists of a spirit and a carbonated soft drink served in a tall glass on ice and garnished with a wedge of lemon. Japanese shochu—a spirit category where the distillates are made from cereals and starches like sweet potato, buckwheat, and barley—is another popular base for highballs, so much so that it has spawned a whole genre of canned flavored cocktails known as chu-hai (a truncation of shochu highball).

Not all Japanese highballs are bubbly, though. The Oolong Hai pairs cold oolong tea and shochu for a drink that is somehow weightless and robust at the same time, expressing the commonalities in flavor shared by the two ingredients. Mugi shochu, distilled from barley, is a match for the fragrant, dry-toasted, grassy qualities of oolong. Without any added sugar or acid in this drink, the tea and spirit are left to shine.

SERVES 1

5 ounces freshly brewed oolong tea, chilled
(brewing instructions follow)

3½ ounces shochu

GARNISH

Dehydrated lemon wheel
(page 24)

HAVE HANDY

Cubed ice

Stack ice in a highball glass nearly to the top. Add the chilled tea and shochu, and briefly stir. Garnish with a dehydrated lemon wheel.

BREWED OOLONG TEA

- To yield 10 ounces of tea, start by heating 2 cups of filtered water in a kettle or small pot and bring to a boil. While the water is warming up, add 4 teaspoons of loose-leaf oolong tea to your steeping vessel, such as a teapot or a large heatproof measuring cup. Once the water comes to a boil, remove from the heat and let it cool briefly, allowing the temperature to decrease to 180 to 200°F. Pour a generous 10 ounces of water over the leaves, and let steep for 3 to 5 minutes, to your taste (a longer steeping time will result in stronger tea). Strain out the solids and run through a coffee filter if needed. Let the tea cool completely before use, or store in a sealed container in the refrigerator for up to 2 weeks.

Bellini

PEACH PUREE & PROSECCO

Like the icy-cool Sgroppino (page 42), the swank Bellini is a gift from Venice, Italy. It's become a brunchtime favorite thanks to its combination of stone fruit—white peach, traditionally—and prosecco. The drink was first served at the iconic Venice landmark Harry's Bar and is named after one of the city's most beloved artists—Renaissance painter Giovanni Bellini.

Prosecco was a natural choice for this lighthearted cocktail, since this variety of sparkler hails primarily from the wine-growing regions of northwest Italy that surround Venice. Some Bellini recipes call for peach nectar, which is peach juice with water and sugar added. Giuseppe Cipriani Sr., the founder of Harry's Bar and the drink's inventor, used pureed ripe white peaches, giving the Bellini a blushing-pink color. Store-bought peach nectar requires no prep (besides chilling) and is finer in texture than a puree; however, you may find it makes for a more cloying Bellini. Fresh fruit, especially in summer, is the move to get that palate-pleasing, naturally candied flavor of ripe peach.

SERVES 1

2 ounces Peach Puree (recipe follows), chilled

4 ounces prosecco, chilled

GARNISH
Peach slice

Add the Peach Puree to a chilled champagne flute or coupe glass. Add about half of the prosecco and gently stir to incorporate. Top with the remaining prosecco. Garnish with a slice of peach on the rim of the glass.

PEACH PUREE

Peach Puree can be made from fresh or frozen peaches. If using fresh, be sure the fruit is ripe for optimal peachiness and adequate sugar content. Two or three peaches will yield enough puree for four Bellinis. Boil the peaches submerged in water for 1 minute, then transfer them into an ice bath. Once cooled, slit the skin, then hand-peel the peaches. Split each and remove the pit. Blend the peaches until smooth, adding a little water if needed. Chill before serving. If using frozen peaches, allow them to thaw, then blend them, adding water if necessary. Refrigerate for up to 1 week.

Rebujito

SHERRY & LEMON-LIME SODA

OFF-DRY, FRESH & DYNAMIC | COLLINS

In Andalucia, home of the fortified wine we call sherry, the Rebujito reigns all through the hot months. This thirst-quenching, ultra-low-ABV drink consists of a combination of dry-style sherry and lemon-lime soda, commonly garnished with a bouquet of mint. (Is this drink by and large a wine spritzer? Yes, it is. Are we okay with that? Yes, we are.) The region reaches peak Rebujito season during the town of Seville's Feria de Abril, a long-standing annual festival that welcomes the arrival of spring.

All of the above signals "porch drink" to me. It's unfussy, sessionable, and is only going to taste better in the open air. For those who are newer to sherry, it can be daunting to grasp the breadth of types and flavor profiles available within the category. There are highly oxidized, raisin-y, concentrated sherries. There are pale, dry, biscuit-y sherries. What's more, the prices vary a lot. This Rebujito provides a breezy way in, calling for either manzanilla or fino, two sherry expressions that are both relatively approachable and affordable for the category.

SERVES 1
3 ounces sherry, preferably manzanilla or fino
6 ounces lemon-lime soda

GARNISH
Mint sprig

HAVE HANDY
Cubed ice

Add the sherry to a chilled Collins glass. Stand a barspoon in the glass and pour the lemon-lime soda down the neck, filling the glass three-quarters to the top. Carefully add ice to fill. Gently slap the mint with the back of your hand to release its aroma. Rest the mint on the surface of the drink.

NOTE
- With some varieties of sherry, such as oloroso and amontillado, oxidation is considered a feature, not a flaw. It's encouraged in the winemaking process to bring out nutty, umami dimensions. "Fresher" sherry varieties like fino, called for here, are shielded from oxidation as they're aged so don't exhibit as much oxidative character. Go ahead and refrigerate fino sherry after opening to mitigate oxidation and finish an open bottle within 3 months. Those heavily oxidized sherries? They'll keep for years.

Lillet & Tonic
LILLET BLANC & TONIC WATER
BRIGHT, FRUITY & FLORAL | COLLINS

You may see Lillet Blanc, the iconic French aperitif, sometimes referred to as an example of *tonic wine*, a term I just love. It sounds healing and delicious, doesn't it? Made in a town south of Bourdeaux, Lillet Blanc is born out of wine made from a blend of Semillon and Sauvignon Blanc grapes. The makers guard specifics of the recipe, but the wine is thought to undergo an infusion with sweet and bitter oranges, then fortification with fruit liqueurs to up the alcohol content and round out the flavor.

Bitter quinine—derived from the bark of the cinchona tree and a key ingredient in tonic water—was once a pronounced component of Lillet Blanc's bittersweet (and now discontinued) predecessor, Kina Lillet. The contemporary formulation of Lillet Blanc seemingly contains little to no quinine, but that dry bitterness still pairs nicely with Lillet Blanc's honeyed-orange notes. So, it's only natural to reintroduce that bitter dimension with a glug of fresh, fizzy tonic water. When you are lazing around on a weekend afternoon and contemplating if it's too early an hour to tuck into a cocktail, a Lillet & Tonic answers that debate quite handily.

SERVES 1

2 ounces Lillet Blanc

5 ounces tonic water, preferably dry in style, such as Q or Top Note

GARNISH

Orange slice
(see page 24 to use up your extra citrus)

HAVE HANDY

Cubed ice

Add the Lillet to a chilled Collins glass. Stand a barspoon in the glass and pour the tonic water down the neck, filling the glass three-quarters to the top. Gently add ice to fill. Tuck in an orange slice.

ENHANCEMENTS & DEPARTURES

* A great number of aperitif wines, including vermouth, sherry, and Cocchi Americano—which many drinkers say is similar in taste to Kina Lillet—will go well with tonic water. Experiment with different products, using the 2:5 ratio as a template.

NOTE

* Because Lillet Blanc is wine based, it will begin to oxidize once opened. This means the character and flavor, even its color, will change over time. This can transform the flavor in interesting ways, but eventually you're likely to no longer like it. Refrigerate after opening to slow down oxidation, and try to use within 3 months.

Mountain Suze

SUZE & MOUNTAIN DEW

Highballs most commonly combine a spirit with soda. Bartenders and drinkers alike have been experimenting with this duo for ages. Some caught fire; others fizzled out. You'd think that every permutation was trialed long ago, but you'd be underestimating the ingenuity of today's cocktail bartenders, and their keenness for upending convention. In recent years a fresh groundswell of slightly transgressive highballs has emerged, pairing genteel cocktail ingredients with uncouth representatives of Big Soda.

Mountain Suze is one of these modern "oddball" experiments that won over even the most pristine cocktail drinkers. It was created at a 2021 barbecue by Sother Teague, whose iconic New York City cocktail bar Amor y Amargo has helped introduce innumerable bargoers to the world of bitter spirits. The drink is a combo of Suze, the French-made bitter liqueur and Mountain Dew, the soft drink born in 1940s Tennessee whose early tagline was "It'll tickle your innards." But the high-sugar, high-caffeine soda—marketed today as a quasi-energy drink—is no stranger to hooch. With its strong lemon-lime flavor, Mountain Dew was originally developed to be mixed with moonshine.

SERVES 1

2 ounces Suze
6 ounces Mountain Dew, or to taste, chilled

HAVE HANDY

Ice cubes

Stack ice in a highball glass nearly to the top. Add the Suze and briefly stir with a barspoon. Stand the barspoon in the glass and pour the Mountain Dew down the neck. Stir again to combine.

NOTE

- Suze, around since 1889, is flavored with yellow gentian root, creating this soft, lingering play between bitter-herb and floral notes.

Sgroppino
LEMON SORBET & PROSECCO
CREAMY, COOLING & TART | COUPE

Hot days call for sorbets! The Italian invention known as Sgroppino recasts this icy dessert as an adult beverage. (Well, an adult who's young at heart.) It's a simple combination of lemon sorbet and prosecco, the Italian sparkling wine, whisked into a frothy slush. Sgroppino is bubbly, lemony, and as pastel yellow as a sunbeam—it really sells itself. Recipes for Sgroppino typically call for vodka and/or limoncello, as well, to provide more alcoholic oomph, but I am often content to enjoy it in this low-ABV format.

The name Sgroppino plays off *sgropin,* a term in the gruff Venetian language meaning loosen or untie. Those who eat too much at dinner might partake in a Sgroppino to help unwind a knotted stomach, treating this cooling beverage like a digestive aid. It is also taken as a palate cleanser between courses of a meal. But I think you'll readily come up with your own reasons (excuses?) to whip up Sgroppino more often—and outside the confines of dining. A dry, citrus-forward prosecco is a desirable option here. Sorbet tends to be quite sugary, so a wine with less of its own sweetness to contribute will yield a more balanced Sgroppino.

SERVES 1

4 tablespoons (2 ounces) lemon sorbet

4 ounces prosecco, chilled

GARNISH

Lemon zest (see page 24 to use up your extra citrus)

Combine the lemon sorbet and 2 ounces of the prosecco in a chilled mixing bowl, whisking until smooth. Add the mixture to a chilled coupe. Add the remaining prosecco. Garnish with lemon zest.

ENHANCEMENTS & DEPARTURES

- For a stiffer Sgroppino, add 1 ounce of chilled vodka to the whisked mixture.

Gin & "Tonic"

GIN & BONAL GENTIANE-QUINA

The Gin & Tonic belongs to the rarefied category of cocktails whose names are the recipes. The G&T is ubiquitous, foolproof . . . it's really not meant to be fussed over or deconstructed. Well, I did say we'd break some rules, so how about a Gin & Tonic without any tonic? Stay with me. The dominant flavoring of tonic water is quinine, which is found naturally in the bark of the South American cinchona tree. Quinine has been taken for medicinal purposes for centuries, and alcohol has always been a popular vehicle to consume it with.

In my tinkering with the Gin & Tonic, a drink that has been one of my go-tos for ages, I found that forgoing tonic water in favor of Bonal Gentiane-Quina—a variety of quinquina formulated by a French Carthusian monk in 1865—and a splash of club soda makes for a more complex, more bracing beverage. The presence of the Bonal balances out even the most vocal gin. I call it the Gin & "Tonic," and it's the drink I want in arm's reach as I cook a big dinner, particularly in summer. Above all, it's cooling. It stimulates your appetite and can stand up to dilution. And with its acid-dry finish, it doesn't linger on your palate for long, like the easy goodbye you share with an old friend, knowing you'll be meeting again soon.

SERVES 1

2 ounces gin
1 ounce Bonal

GARNISH

Lime wedge
(see page 24 to use up your extra citrus)

HAVE HANDY

Cubed ice
Club soda

Add the gin and Bonal to a chilled Collins glass and briefly stir. Stand a barspoon in the glass and pour the club soda down the neck, filling the glass three-quarters to the top. Gently add ice to fill. Squeeze the lime wedge over the glass and add to the beverage.

ENHANCEMENTS & DEPARTURES

- A brash and challenging alternative to the conventional G&T is to explore the category of clairin in place of the gin. Clairin is a fragrant, funky Haitian spirit brimming with ripe fruit flavors, often made from heirloom varieties of sugarcanes. Many clairin makers bottle their goods without any dilution, in the ballpark of 50 percent ABV, so a little goes a long way. A Clairin & Tonic is big, aromatic, and spirit-forward—a dazzler for your palate.

Absinthe Coconut Frappé

ABSINTHE VERTE & CREAM OF COCONUT

LUSCIOUS, LICORICE & BEACHY | FRAPPÉ OR HIGHBALL

I've been a fan of the unlikely pairing of absinthe and coconut since I first tried the inventive Absinthe Colada—a play on the Piña Colada—at Brooklyn's Maison Premiere. It's the rare cocktail bar that venerates absinthe's exquisiteness. Absinthe geeks can choose from a deep list of imported and domestic bottles and enjoy them in the traditional manner: chilled water is gradually dripped onto a pour of absinthe from a fountain, through a sugar cube sitting on a perforated spoon; this opens up the botanicals and softens the edge of the spirit. The introduction of water transmogrifies absinthe verte from a vegetal green to a mesmerizing pearlescent jade, an effect the French call La Louche.

This drink inspired me to experiment with a coconut-sweetened riff on the absinthe frappé, which originated in New Orleans in 1874. The old recipe consists of absinthe and simple syrup bathed in a glassful of chipped ice, topped off with club soda—all the elements of traditional absinthe service, just prepared a little differently. This version uses an easy-to-make Cream of Coconut in place of simple syrup to lend the classic cocktail a tropical dimension—a perfect afternoon pick-me-up.

SERVES 1

1½ ounces
absinthe verte

1 ounce
homemade
Cream of
Coconut
(recipe follows),
**or substitute
canned**

HAVE HANDY

Ice cubes

Chipped ice

Club soda

Add the absinthe and Cream of Coconut to a cocktail shaker. Add ice cubes and shake vigorously for 10 seconds. Strain into a highball glass (or, if you have it, a footed absinthe glass) packed with chipped ice. Top with club soda.

CREAM OF COCONUT

Combine a 14-ounce can of unsweetened full-fat coconut milk and 1 cup of granulated sugar in a medium saucepan. Warm over low heat, stirring occasionally, until the sugar has fully dissolved. Add a pinch of salt. Let the mixture cool, and store in the refrigerator for up to 1 week.

WEEKNI

As the Stranger tells The Dude, "Sometimes you eat the bear . . . Some-times the bear, well, he eats you." On those days when we give our best stuff and life leaves us wound up or winded, a certain breed of drink soothes better than most. Let's call this the Weeknightcap. It's the lazy, consoling lapdog of your home-bar repertoire: perfect for solo sipping or a communal venting session.

When I picture a drink that unwinds on a weeknight, above all it's a comforting companion. In a show of understanding, it mirrors the brooding air I may be exhibiting at the time. Dark, aged, and oth-erwise big-shouldered spirits like whiskey, brandy, absinthe, rum, and amaro serve as a base of these drinks. With a sweet yet faintly medicinal flavor profile, a Weeknightcap supplies a kind of pseudo-therapeutic indulgence, like a candy that masquerades as a lozenge.

Weeknightcaps belong to the class of long drinks, served tall and above average in volume, thus taking a little while to consume—and, hey, who's going to complain about more time spent on indulgence? The alcohol content of the spirit is mellowed by the introduction of a modifier such as a soft drink, tonic, or cider. Because this is not a

HTCAPS

moment to get caught up in ritual, a Weeknightcap—much like The Dude's White Russian—is unfussy in its preparation. Toss it together and you're on a fast track to the couch (or rug) to commiserate, recharge, zone out—whatever you name that act of giving yourself an existential hug.

For those who enjoy the dessert-spice sharpness of ginger, the Scotch drink known by some as the Presbyterian is one to try. If you're like me, the flavor and aroma of apples is an expressway to happy memories, which makes drinks like the Spiced Pear Cider and the classic Stone Fence instantly familiar and blissful. For drinks with an herbal and earthy profile, the Root of All Evil, pairing absinthe and root beer, is a surprisingly delightful place to start. For those evenings where you need a coffee but don't want just a coffee, the restorative, alcohol-free Espresso & Tonic is the answer. And to round out this collection of empathic drinks, of course there are some that taste bittersweet, like the Broke in Bottle. These Weeknightcaps promise comfort and lull but pack all the liveliness you want in a cocktail—perfect if you're not into the whole brevity thing.

Broke in Bottle
CANE SUGAR COCA-COLA & BRUTO AMERICANO

CARAMEL, BALSAM & CLOVE | SODA BOTTLE

Bruto Americano is an American-made amaro that is intensely herbal, with foresty notes like balsam fir and mint. Coca-Cola needs no introduction. Portmanteau 'em, and the mashup of ingredients does wonders. They smooth each other's sharp edges, giving you a drink that is neither overly sweet nor medicinal. Several amaro-plus-Coke combinations work nicely, but I particularly like the balancing act these two perform. I highly recommend you search out the cane sugar variety found in glass bottles—commonly referred to as "Mexican Coca-Cola."

It's soothing. It's slow-sipping. It's treatlike yet feels adult. But if there's one thing beyond all others that makes this a quintessential Week-nightcap, it's the ease of prep, and the Broke in Bottle is the perfect "in a pinch" cocktail to whip up at home or to bring to your next social gathering.

SERVES 1

1 12-ounce glass-bottled cane sugar Coca-Cola, well chilled

2 ounces Bruto Americano

GARNISH

Unpitted medium green olive, such as Castelvetrano (optional)

Open an ice-cold Coke bottle and pour out 2 ounces into a measuring cup. (Feel free to enjoy this bit as an amuse-bouche.) Refill the bottle with the Bruto Americano. To add some flavor-enhancing salinity, plop in a green olive that's just wider than the mouth of the bottle. Use a long straw to first stir, then drink.

Dark & Stormy
GINGER BEER & RUM

FRUITY, FUNKY & SHARP | HIGHBALL

Mules are combinations of a spirit and ginger beer. The Moscow mule is a mule made with vodka. The gin-gin mule is, well, fairly self-explanatory. The rum mule, best known by a different title, the Dark & Stormy, is my favorite of all the quaffable mules. The drink is thought to have originated in Bermuda, and it has always remained synonymous with island life. The crisp, tingly flavor of ginger beer is the canvas, and the rum paints in the color, both literally and figuratively. The name refers to the effect achieved by floating black or dark rum atop the ginger beer, giving the appearance of looming dark clouds.

Gosling's, the Bermudan beverage company, has trademarked its version using the brand's black seal rum and ginger beer. You don't have to reach for a black rum (some can taste artificial), but to create the storm-cloud look, some form of dark rum is a must. This diverse spirits category offers a playground of options, each accentuating your Dark & Stormy in different ways. I go for aged Jamaican rums—commonly exhibiting big, heady aromas of ripe pineapple and banana, vanilla, and burnt sugar—which stand up to the intense spice of a good, dry-style ginger beer.

SERVES 1

4 ounces ginger beer, chilled

2 ounces dark rum, preferably aged Jamaican

GARNISH

Lime wedge
(see page 24 to use up your extra citrus)

HAVE HANDY

Cubed ice

Fill a highball glass with ice. Add the ginger beer. Hold a wide spoon with its face down over the mouth of the glass and slowly pour in the rum so it spreads over the back, floating it on top. Garnish with a lime wedge. After you enjoy the show, stir the contents to incorporate the rum, lest the first sip is ginger beer or rum alone.

ENHANCEMENTS & DEPARTURES

- Squeeze the juice of a lime wedge into the glass after the ginger beer is added for a zippier sip.

- The rum family comprises a big cast of characters, and this is a flexible template through which to explore it. You can split the spirit in a rum mule between different expressions, such as 1 ounce each of light and dark rum, where the light rum is added to the glass first to preserve the classic look.

Filmograph

PEAR BRANDY & KOLA TONIC

TANGY, LIME ZEST & TROPICAL | LOWBALL

The Filmograph is an obscure vintage cocktail that deserves another look. It shows up in *The Savoy Cocktail Book*, a compendium of over 700 drink recipes by bartender Harry Craddock, first released in 1930. There the Filmograph is listed as a shaken drink combining brandy, sirop-de-citron, and kola tonic. Sirop-de-citron is a bittersweet lemon syrup, common back in Craddock's day. Kola tonic is a nonalcoholic, naturally caffeinated beverage whose distinctive flavor (and buzz) comes from the kola nut. (The same nut was the key to Coca-Cola when it first emerged.) Claytons Kola Tonic, produced in Barbados, stands as one of the few remaining purveyors. Its flavor is reminiscent of cola with lime.

So what does the Filmograph look like for the twenty-first century? This interpretation simplifies the build, relying on the inherent sweetness and citric acidity of the contemporary Claytons formula to do the job of the sirop-de-citron. Traditionally, the brandy would have been grape based—most likely a Cognac—but I like pear brandy here, instead. The drink tastes unusual yet oddly familiar. It's comforting in the way cracking into a fruit cup after school was for me as a kid.

SERVES 1
1½ ounces pear brandy
1½ ounces Claytons Kola Tonic

GARNISH
Fresh or dried pineapple

HAVE HANDY
Cubed ice

Add the brandy and kola tonic to a lowball glass. Top with ice, then stir to chill, for about 30 seconds. Garnish with a cube of fresh or dried pineapple on a cocktail skewer.

ENHANCEMENTS & DEPARTURES

- Take the Filmograph into tiki territory by swapping the pear brandy for Lucky Falernum. This product has all the juicy, ginger-lime, and allspice qualities of a traditional falernum syrup, which is used a lot in tiki drink recipes, but at 35 percent ABV it acts like a spirit.

NOTE

- Those familiar with *The Savoy Cocktail Book* might recognize that this twist on the Filmograph takes some inspo from the Elixir Cocktail, which Craddock spec'ed as equal parts kola tonic and Calvados, the apple brandy from Normandy, France.
- To stretch this drink out, serve in an ice-filled highball glass for an extra cooling sip.

Espresso & Tonic
TONIC WATER & ESPRESSO
BROODING, CHOCOLATEY & EFFERVESCENT | LOWBALL

There's a saying in tech, "a solution in search of a problem," that describes products and advancements that superficially seem exciting and innovative but, in actuality, aren't alleviating any real challenges. Espresso & Tonic is the opposite: not nearly enough of our problems are seeking out this beverage for help.

A simple pairing of fresh espresso and tonic water over ice, an E&T drinks like a cocktail but has no alcohol (a nice thing to have in your repertoire of Weeknightcaps). The unctuousness and metallic intensity of espresso's acidity are dialed down to a hum thanks to the tonic. Nuanced flavors in the coffee become more accessible. It's an iced coffee that's less jittery than cold brew. And, with no milk, an Espresso & Tonic doesn't leave you feeling full. It's the perfect evening brew.

SERVES 1

3 ounces tonic water, chilled

2 ounces espresso (a double shot), left to cool

GARNISH

Orange wheel (see page 24 to use up your extra citrus)

HAVE HANDY

Cubed ice

Fill a lowball glass with ice and add the tonic water. Pour in the espresso and briefly stir. Tuck in an orange wheel.

ENHANCEMENTS & DEPARTURES

- Newer tonic waters are trending drier these days, so you may wish to introduce an additional sweetening agent to your Espresso & Tonic, such as Homemade Vanilla Syrup (start with ½ ounce, adjusting to taste). To make the syrup, split a vanilla bean pod lengthwise and scrape out the seeds. Combine the vanilla husk, seeds, and 1 cup each of water and granulated sugar in a saucepan over medium heat. Once the sugar is dissolved, let cool. Strain before bottling and storing in the fridge for up to 2 weeks. (As an aesthetic choice, you can opt to coffee-filter out the fine particles, but note that the espresso is going to obscure them.) For a spirited sweetener, try triple sec, the orange liqueur that flavors a classic Margarita.

Stone Fence

APPLE BRANDY & SPARKLING HARD CIDER

I'm from the Northeast, so of course I love a good old stone fence. I'm also a fan of the cocktail by the same name, which is all about enjoying another Northeast staple: the apple. A simple combination of apple brandy and hard apple cider, the Stone Fence is intertwined with American history. A Scotsman, Alexander Laird, came to what is now New Jersey in the late 1600s and went on to produce apple brandy using fruit from local trees. The Laird family counted general-turned-president George Washington as a customer, and Stone Fences are thought to have steeled the Green Mountain Boys militia during the Revolutionary War. I can report that after 200-plus years, the Stone Fence still works to calm the nerves. And it's bound to stir nostaglia for cherished apple pies of yore. (Yore welcome.)

American apple brandy has re-surged after receding during the twentieth century, giving drinkers today a wealth of options. The Laird family is still at it, and are now joined by many other distillers tapping into the national bounty of apples. For the hard apple cider, I like dryish-style sparkling varieties. You can stay domestic, or seek out lovely European examples like cuvée cider from Italian producer Melchiori.

SERVES 1

2 ounces apple brandy, such as Laird's

4 ounces hard sparkling apple cider, chilled

GARNISH

Apple slice

HAVE HANDY

Cubed ice

Fill a highball glass with ice and add the apple brandy. Pour the cider down the neck of a barspoon. Briefly stir. Tuck in an apple slice.

The Root of All Evil

ABSINTHE VERTE & ROOT BEER

BOLD, SPICY-SWEET & COOLING | LOWBALL

Some absinthe cocktails shimmer like Venus carved in marble. Their alluring color—born from the luminous glow that comes when the spirit is diluted—is a visual prelude to their verdant alpine taste. This particular absinthe drink, however, isn't quite so beautiful. In fact, this cocktail is a little murky. While its looks are not the strong suit of this drink, the Root of All Evil (alluding to the old and thoroughly debunked claims that absinthe is dangerously psychoactive) more than makes up for that in taste.

Ellie Winters of St. George Spirits—a California distillery that was the first in the US to produce an American absinthe after the country's so-called ban on the spirit was lifted in 2007—stumbled upon this simpatico combination. The distillery's preferred version goes light on the root beer, with 2 ounces; I like to add a bit more here. The two ingredients working well together shouldn't be all that surprising: they have common flavor profiles, including fresh mint and anise. This is a great drink for the absinthe-curious; the earthy, spicy, dark-sugar qualities of root beer provide a familiar, comfortable entry point, like grabbing a stool at the counter of a classic diner.

SERVES 1

1 ounce
St. George
Absinthe Verte

4 ounces root
beer, such as
Virgil's

GARNISH

Star anise pod

HAVE HANDY

Cubed ice

Pour the absinthe into a lowball glass filled with ice and top off with a good-quality root beer. Gradually let louche (pronounced "loosh"; see Note), stirring gently until the drink looks cloudy. Garnish with a star anise pod.

NOTE

▪ How do you "let louche"? You could hit the discotheque and just dance like nobody's watching. But in this case we're talking terpenes. Spirits like absinthe and pastis are rich in terpenes: hydrocarbon molecules that come from the plant life used to flavor them, including anise, fennel, and wormwood. These molecules readily dissolve when bathed in high concentrations of ethanol. But if that concentration of ethanol drops through dilution—root beer–based or otherwise—below a certain threshold, then the terpenes can no longer hide. They come out of solution, appearing as a pearly, translucent haze.

Presbyterian
SCOTCH & GINGER ALE

It's not uncommon for drinks to get "invented" many times over. Bartenders have always acted as tastemakers and trend-chasers, such that more than one can reach the same original idea, unbeknownst to the other. Hence the annals of mixed drinks that are chock-full of close (or identical) iterations. A whiskey-ginger highball is a prime example.

A drink named after Broadway star Mayme Taylor called the Mamie Taylor (yes, the misspelled homage has gone uncorrected) includes Scotch, ginger beer, and lime. The Horse's Neck is a cocktail that typically features American whiskey, ginger ale, and a superlong citrus peel ringing the inside wall of the glass. Seated in between those two is the Presbyterian, which arose in Scotland as a combination of blended Scotch whisky and ginger ale, topped with club soda.

Opt for this instance of whiskey-meets-ginger when you're after something mellow and easy-drinking. When unwinding with a generously carbonated Presbyterian, I don't dwell much on whether I should or shouldn't go back for seconds.

SERVES 1

2 ounces blended Scotch whisky

2 ounces ginger ale, chilled

GARNISH

Candied ginger

HAVE HANDY

Cubed ice

Club soda

Fill a highball glass with ice. Add the Scotch, then the ginger ale, pouring it down your barspoon. Gently stir to mix. Add 2 ounces of club soda. Garnish with a piece of candied ginger on a cocktail skewer.

ENHANCEMENTS & DEPARTURES

- Experiment with throwing in a couple of dashes of Angostura bitters to your Presbyterian to add a woodsy dimension that plays well with the charred-oak notes of the Scotch.

Amaro & Chinotto
ITALIAN AMARO & CHINOTTO SODA

BITTER ORANGE & HERBS | LOWBALL

Here we have amaro, the Italian bitter liqueur, paired with chinotto, the Italian bitter soda. You might reasonably expect the outcome to taste like bitterness squared, but that's seldom what happens when cocktails call for multiple bitter ingredients. Instead of trying to talk over each other, they tend to harmonize.

Chinotto is made from the fruit of *Citrus myrtifolia,* the myrtle-leaved orange tree. The little oranges it produces, called *chinotti* in Italian, are bitter and sour. The bubbly soda's brownish color—akin to cola—belies flavors of candied, aromatic orange peel. The same fruit is used in a host of amari, offering a point of intersection between the two that helps make this drink work beautifully.

SERVES 1

2 ounces amaro, such as Meletti

4 ounces chinotto

GARNISH

Orange slice
(see page 24 to use up your extra citrus)

HAVE HANDY

Cubed ice

Fill a lowball glass with ice and add the amaro. Pour the chinotto down the neck of a barspoon. Briefly stir. Tuck in an orange slice.

Spiced Pear Cider

APPLE CIDER & SPICED PEAR LIQUEUR

NOURISHING, JUICY & TART | TODDY GLASS OR MUG

If you've fallen for the crisp and cooling, apple-tastic Stone Fence (page 58), you may be asking yourself, *but what do I do in winter?* Let me put your mind at ease. The answer is this Spiced Pear Cider—a roaring fire of a beverage, capable of warming up cold, dark evenings.

This recipe comes by way of St. George Spirits, which produces a spiced pear liqueur made from Bartlett pears. Steamy hot apple cider (the orchard-style—cloudy and dark) teams up with pear liqueur to upgrade a wintertime favorite, perfect for a solo slow sipper on a chilly day. Like many of these recipes, you can scale up the amounts to make multiple cocktails, and the Spiced Pear Cider is the perfect group indulgence.

SERVES 1

4 ounces apple cider

2 ounces St. George Spiced Pear Liqueur

GARNISH

Cinnamon stick

Heat the apple cider and pour into a mug or toddy glass. Add the pear liqueur and briefly stir. Garnish with a cinnamon stick.

DRINK
NIBE

Tucked somewhere between the meals of lunch and dinner is a splendid way of life called aperitivo. It's an Italian word (the French equivalent is *aperitif*) commonly applied to beverages, but it also signifies the long-held ritual that surrounds them—one of celebrating pure leisure.

Usually moderate in alcohol and a tad bitter, apertivi stimulate your appetite and are typically served alongside casual snack foods like olives, cheeses, and even salty potato chips. It's thought that this prelude to the larger meal cues the body to jump-start digestion, lessening the risk of your gut feeling bloated later on.

The modern traditions associated with aperitivo coalesced in late 1700s Torino and its dynamic café culture. Picture afternoons spilling into evenings, guests strolling into chic establishments to socialize. Aperitivo grew to mean not only a convivial gathering but also a mutual agreement to linger on the corner we turn between our day and evening selves. It stands apart from the happy hour and its commercial undertones—aperitivo shuns the very thought of a schedule.

ING & LING

The aperitivo canon encompasses many types of beverages under the unofficial grouping of augmented wines. Barolo chinato, quinquina, sherry, and, above all, vermouth are among the best-known examples. All of these can be sipped on their own, and pretty much all of them also work well—and work well together—in cocktails. A host of bitter liqueurs also find their way into aperitivo cocktails—Campari and Aperol being two examples that immediately come to mind. Gin is perhaps the spirit most associated with aperitivo; an under-the-radar aperitivo is Pink Gin, in which the botanical spirit is seasoned with bitters. For a stiffer sip, look to the Martini-like Tuxedo, a blend of gin and sherry. Following suit is the Americano, a combination of sweet vermouth and bitter Campari, served fizzy with seltzer. And yes, of course, we'll explore the Spritz in all its bittersweet and bubbly glory. I say we invite in the aperitivo. Your heart, belly, and brain will thank you.

Spritz

APEROL & PROSECCO

My first and most indelible exposure to the gracious lifestyle surrounding aperitivo came in Venice, Italy, where strolling and boating are the prevailing modes of transportation. To roam between pocket-size taverns called *bacari*, which ply you with *ombra* (diminutive cups of wine) and *cicchetti* (Venice's version of tapas), is a popular pursuit.

For a drink and a nibble all in one bittersweet and savory package, you can reach for a Spritz, adorned in the Venetian manner with an orange slice and a few plump green olives. I could watch sunlight pass through its candied-orange prism all afternoon. (And indeed I have. You should try it, too.) The mildly bitter-orange backbone of Aperol and the dryness of prosecco give the Spritz just enough heft and character to offset its sweetness, keeping this drink from being cloying.

For me, the Spritz is a casual drink and calls for a casual snack to go with it. Really salty potato chips are a go-to, although I wouldn't turn down a parmesan crisp.

SERVES 1

2 ounces Aperol

4 ounces prosecco, chilled

GARNISHES

Green olives, unpitted, such as Castelvetrano

Orange slice
(see page 24 to use up your extra citrus)

HAVE HANDY

Cubed ice

Seltzer

Add the Aperol to a lowball or wineglass. Nearly fill it with ice. Pour the prosecco down the neck of a barspoon. Add a splash of seltzer. To garnish, drop in 2 or 3 unpitted green olives and tuck in an orange slice.

71

Adonis

SHERRY & VERMOUTH

TOFFEE, DATES & COCOA | COUPE OR NICK & NORA

This and the next drink, the Bamboo (page 75), are like siblings. Both are combinations of sherry and vermouth. Whereas the Bamboo is a drier, more herbal cocktail, the Adonis is rounder and sweeter.

You could mistake this drink for a Manhattan, thanks to the pairing of sweet vermouth and cream sherry (not the traditional choice of sherry, but to my liking), yet it isn't nearly as strong. So, the Adonis enables you to sip on a flavorful, fragrant stirred cocktail without worrying you'll be weighted down (or wobbly) after drinking it.

Complementing a round or two of Adonises (Adonii?) with a selection of dried fruits and salted nuts is an easy way to elevate your aperitivo hour by accentuating the raisin notes and salinity in the sherry.

SERVES 1

1½ ounces cream sherry, preferably Lustau East India Solera

1½ ounces sweet vermouth, preferably Punt e Mes

GARNISH

Lemon twist
(see page 24 to use up your extra citrus)

HAVE HANDY

Cubed ice

Add the sherry and vermouth to a mixing glass. Add ice and stir for 15 seconds. Strain into a chilled coupe or Nick & Nora glass. Express the lemon twist over the glass and discard.

ENHANCEMENTS & DEPARTURES

- If this take on the Adonis is too muscular for your tastes, revert to the drink's traditional build—made by pairing a drier-style sherry, like fino, with a milder sweet vermouth, then adding in a couple of dashes of orange bitters—for a softer sip.

Bamboo

SHERRY & VERMOUTH

HONEY, BLACK TEA & ORANGE BLOSSOMS | COUPE OR NICK & NORA

On the heels of the Adonis (page 72), we add to the wine-on-wine action with the Bamboo, a duo of dry sherry and dry vermouth. The Bamboo is as mellow as a Zen garden, perfect for an aperitivo hour that is designed around softer flavors, so consider setting out some green grapes and mild cheeses alongside this cocktail.

Unlike many aperitivo cocktails, this one doesn't trace back to Europe. History records the Bamboo as coming into its own at the turn of the twentieth century when it was a signature drink of bartender Louis Eppinger while he was posted at the bar of the Grand Hotel in Yokohama, Japan.

SERVES 1

1½ ounces amontillado sherry, such as Valdespino Tio Diego

1½ ounces dry vermouth, such as Dolin

GARNISH

Lemon twist
(see page 24 to use up your extra citrus)

HAVE HANDY

Cubed ice

Add the sherry and vermouth to a mixing glass. Add ice and stir for 15 seconds. Strain into a chilled coupe or Nick & Nora glass. Express the lemon twist over the glass and discard.

ENHANCEMENTS & DEPARTURES

- Add 2 dashes of orange bitters into the mixing glass along with the sherry and vermouth to further accentuate the citrus notes.

Pink Gin

GIN & BITTERS

As a general rule, aperitivo cocktails shouldn't be complicated to build. We are attempting to be decidedly off-the-clock during this time, after all. If there's a role model showing others how to be an easygoing, easy-making aperitivo cocktail, the utterly uncomplicated Pink Gin is it.

This stirred drink is composed of London dry gin, seasoned with Angostura bitters (which turns the clear gin rosy). The bitters sing backup to the juniper-scented lead vocals of the gin.

For the accompanying nibble, look to dark fresh fruits like figs and raspberries. The latter is well known to be friendly with gin; they get together in a cocktail called the Clover Club.

SERVES 1

2 ounces London dry gin

4 dashes Angostura bitters

GARNISH

Lemon twist
(see page 24 to use up your extra citrus)

HAVE HANDY

Cubed ice

Add the gin to a mixing glass. Dash in the bitters. Add ice and stir for 30 seconds. Strain into an ice-filled lowball glass. Garnish with a lemon twist.

ENHANCEMENTS & DEPARTURES

- Another way to make this drink is with Old Tom, a sweeter, richer style of gin, rather than London dry.

- Once the classic Pink Gin formulation hooks you in, why not try this cocktail with Peychaud's bitters in lieu of Angostura for more of a licorice-like hint?

Carajillo
ESPRESSO & LICOR 43

VANILLA, CHOCOLATE & BITTER LEMON | LOWBALL

Aperitivo hour is meant to prime your stomach and recalibrate your mindset in anticipation of a long, leisurely dinner. If you feel your energy is flagging and worry that a heavy meal will deliver a knockout blow to your evening, the Carajillo may be the secret potion that revives you. It's the simple combination of espresso and Licor 43, a distinctive liqueur from Spain with a prominent vanilla and citrus character (forty-three ingredients are said to give it its flavor).

In terms of food pairings, look to treats where sweet is the suffix—bittersweet dark chocolate, savory-sweet peanut brittle—so as to play off the nuances in the coffee and liqueur.

SERVES 1

2 ounces espresso
(a double shot),
left to cool

1½ ounces
Licor 43

GARNISH

Lemon twist
(see page 24 to use up
your extra citrus)

HAVE HANDY

Cubed ice

Add the espresso and Licor 43 to a cocktail shaker with ice. Shake for 10 seconds. Strain into an ice filled lowball glass. Garnish with a lemon twist.

ENHANCEMENTS & DEPARTURES

- The Carajillo can also be enjoyed warm: simply mix the fresh, hot espresso and Licor 43 in a lowball glass. Garnish with a lemon twist, and/or a sprinkle of cinnamon for an extra warming touch.

Americano

CAMPARI & VERMOUTH

GRAPEFRUIT PITH & CHERRY COLA | HIGHBALL

This bubbly, highball-format aperitivo is Italian through and through, despite the name. Equal parts Campari and sweet Italian vermouth work so nicely together (see also: Negroni), and here the duo is left to shine on its own. And if you and your friends prefer to take your Americanos in more "saluti!"-appropriate stemmed glassware, that's cool, too.

With the inclusion of seltzer, the Americano is juicy and full-flavored yet buoyant. (Subtract the seltzer and you have a Milano-Torino cocktail.) Cater your Americanos as you would a pleasure-boat cruise along the Amalfi coast—with crumbly aged cheeses, cured meats, olives, and other savory foods that get you into the rhythm of sip, nibble, sip, nibble . . .

SERVES 1

1½ ounces Campari

1½ ounces sweet vermouth, such as Cocchi Vermouth di Torino

GARNISH

Lemon slice (see page 24 to use up your extra citrus)

HAVE HANDY

Cubed ice

Seltzer

Add the Campari and sweet vermouth to a chilled highball glass. Add ice to nearly fill the glass. Top with seltzer. Briefly stir to mix. Tuck in a lemon slice.

ENHANCEMENTS & DEPARTURES

- If accessible, swap in a blood orange slice for the lemon garnish.

- Torinese sweet vermouth is very typical, but I encourage you to experiment with alternatives. Vermut Negre is a beautifully nutty, concentrated, sweet-style vermouth from Spain; Casa Mariol's is a great introduction.

- For a more alpine vibe, change out the vermouth for the smoky, spruce-y Amaro Pasubio. Unlike the majority of amari, which have a spirit base, Pasubio is a vino amaro—an amaro where the alcohol content comes from wine—making it a suitable sub for vermouth.

Tuxedo

GIN & SHERRY

A few very different drinks go by the name Tuxedo. No surprise it's a popular moniker, since it conveys classiness. *This* Tuxedo cocktail, combining gin and dry-style sherry, has a similar bearing to that of a Martini, so the name feels apt. In its flavor profile it diverges, though, with more of a savory streak than the Martini's bright botanical essence.

A plate of freshly shucked oysters wouldn't last long in the presence of a few Tuxedos, nor would a couple of baguettes' worth of the Spanish favorite pan con tomate. The brininess of the shellfish and the brightness of the tomatoes draw a straight line to the sherry's inherent salinity and acidity. Do your best to mind your slurping and crunching sounds to keep it classy.

SERVES 1

2 ounces London dry gin

1 ounce sherry, preferably fino

GARNISH

Orange twist
(see page 24 to use up your extra citrus)

HAVE HANDY

Cubed ice

Add the gin and sherry to a mixing glass. Add ice and stir for 30 seconds. Strain into a chilled coupe or Nick & Nora glass. Express the orange twist over the glass and drop it in.

NOTE

- Optionally, you can add 2 dashes of orange bitters along with the gin and sherry for a nice bitter, citrusy flare.

CELEBI
LIBAT

We don't talk nearly enough about the blessing that is bubbles. For those of us who enjoy the bracing tingle of carbonation on our tongues, we should count ourselves incredibly fortunate that the universe's innumerable dice rolls led to conditions here on Earth where, firstly, carbon dioxide gas readily dissolves into water and ethanol; and secondly, our ingestion of said liquids provokes surprise and delight. And that feeling never gets old.

Research has shown that our perception of carbonation in beverages is attributable to the physical sensation of bursting bubbles, as carbon dioxide gas flees its liquid confines. But that's only part of the equation. The experience of that telltale tingle isn't just our perception of the bubbles doing their thing. Humans have adapted the facility, through an enzyme that lives on our tongues, to register the carbonic acid present in carbonated beverages as a sharp, almost singeing, sourness. One theory is that we acquired this adaptation as a warning system against spoiled food and drink. I think our love affair with bubbly beverages is wrapped up in the way the carbonation intrigues our palates—physiologically and biochemically.

Maybe deep down in our animal wiring we pick up on the potential danger. Regardless, carbonation heightens our attention, it firms our grasp on the present. To me it's no coincidence, therefore, that celebratory cocktails are often bubbly ones. When we come together to observe something special—a marriage, a birthday, a new job, a new home—we want to encourage our senses to fire, to flood them with stimulation, so in turn the most vivid pictures of the moment are imprinted on our memories.

Not all drinks cataloged here are effervescent; I'm not arguing that carbonation is a prerequisite for a party drink, but each one possesses a similar power to reorient us toward full hearts, laughter, and joy. Some might do so by offering a taste of luxury (i.e., fancy drinks like the Kir Royale). Others foster effortless social cohesion (cherished, celebratory drinks like the Cuba Libre). Some belong to the living folklore of communities (familiar drinks like the Bicicletta). These drinks are comfortable in banquet halls and backyards alike. In short, they cheers a little different. Let's celebrate that.

Champagne Cocktail
BITTERED SUGAR & CHAMPAGNE

TOASTED BRIOCHE, CARAMEL & LEMON | FLUTE

The French have an enviable vocabulary to describe the bubbles in their wine. Champagne exhibits *perlage,* when carbonation escapes through delicate bubbles that resemble strings of tiny pearls. The word *mousse* is inseparable from the term *mousseux,* which means sparkling and is applied to carbonated wine. I delight in thinking about the textual/textural connections created by using overlapping terminology for an airy, whipped dessert and a frothy, chewy sparkling wine.

The Champagne Cocktail, which originated in the mid-1800s, takes Champagne and makes it sweeter, more playful, and livelier. A bitters-soaked sugar cube provides a dose of bittersweetness that gradually releases into the drink (only dissolving somewhat), as well as a nucleation site—a craggy surface where CO_2 can gather and form bubbles.

SERVES 1

1 brown sugar cube

5 ounces Champagne, chilled

GARNISH

Lemon twist
(optional) (see page 24 to use up your extra citrus)

HAVE HANDY

Angostura bitters

Add the sugar cube to a chilled Champagne flute so it rests at the bottom. Soak the cube with 5 to 6 dashes of bitters. Gradually pour in the Champagne. Hang a lemon twist off the rim of the glass, if using.

ENHANCEMENTS & DEPARTURES

- There are many types of Champagne—from Brut (the driest) to Doux (the sweetest). By simply changing the style of Champagne, you can create an impressive range of cocktails. Experiment with different levels of sweetness to find your preferred balance alongside the bitters. Champagnes that show off the category's yeasty biscuit flavors, which arise from the fermentation methods used, are a great choice for this cocktail.

- Add 1 ounce of ice-cold Cognac following the sugar cube and bitters for an extra, toasted dimension.

Perfect Sake Martini

SAKE & GIN

I'm not calling this cocktail perfect in any self-congratulatory way. In the realm of mixed drinks, "perfect" is a term applied to ingredients in equal measure. A "perfect" Manhattan would have the same amounts of whiskey and sweet vermouth, for example. So, this Perfect Sake Martini is equal portions of sake and gin. Sake is made from the fermentation of rice. Humble as it sounds, sake is an incredibly diverse beverage category with a range of expressions that seem implausible given the raw materials. From flower-petal delicate to grain-bowl savory, sake provides a bounty of options to choose from.

This cocktail is an opportunity to tap into each ingredient's complexity and connect the dots of flavor. Citrus-forward gins can find kinship in tartly acidic sakes, whereas more nuanced botanical gins may work well for the cleaner varieties of sake.

SERVES 1

1½ ounces sake, preferably Junmai

1½ ounces gin, such as Forthave Spirits Blue or The Botanist

GARNISH

Green olive, preferably unpitted Castelvetrano

HAVE HANDY

Cubed ice

Add the sake and gin to a mixing glass. Add ice and stir for 30 seconds. Strain into a chilled coupe or Nick & Nora glass. Drop in the green olive.

ENHANCEMENTS & DEPARTURES

- Because the flavors of this Martini variant are rather delicate, the choice of garnish can exert more influence and nudge the drink into different territories. For a sweeter, fruitier version, go with a peeled lychee on a skewer. A slice of cucumber lends a hint of melon. Or try a piece of umeboshi (Japanese pickled plum) for a little extra brightness.

Bicicletta

WHITE WINE & CAMPARI

CITRUS PEELS & TART GREEN APPLES | LOWBALL

Sometimes cocktails are great because the ingredients are exceptional and only make each other that much better. Historically, the purposes of cocktails were to make not-so-great-tasting spirits (which suffered from rudimentary distilling technology or amateur craftsmanship) taste much more palatable.

Remember that, and this drink, the next time you throw a party and a guest brings over a very run-of-the-mill white wine. It happens. Maybe we've even been that guest. In the Bicicletta, we macrodose ho-hum white wine with bittersweet Campari to give that pale juice more personality.

SERVES 1

3 ounces white wine, such as Pinot Grigio

3 ounces Campari

GARNISH

Orange wheel
(see page 24 to use up your extra citrus)

HAVE HANDY

Cubed ice

Seltzer

Combine the wine and Campari in a chilled lowball glass. Add ice to nearly fill. Add seltzer by pouring down the neck of a barspoon to top. Tuck in an orange wheel.

Death in the Afternoon

ABSINTHE & CHAMPAGNE

LICORICE, APPLE & YEAST | COUPE OR FLUTE

In this cocktail, attached in history to the writer Ernest Hemingway (who wrote a book about bullfighting with the same title), Champagne is modified by a measure of absinthe. What you get is a more herbaceous and big-flavored expression of the French sparkling wine—or, viewed from the opposite angle, a means to drink absinthe where you dilute it with basically the nicest juice you can find.

This is a decadent drink, not for the faint of heart. Consider sweeter expressions of Champagne if you wish to moderate the intensity of the absinthe.

SERVES 1

½ ounce absinthe, such as Pernod

5 ounces Champagne, chilled

GARNISH

Lemon twist
(see page 24 to use up your extra citrus)

Add the absinthe to a chilled glass. Gradually pour in the Champagne. Hang a lemon twist off the rim of the glass.

ENHANCEMENTS & DEPARTURES

- A variation on this drink uses sparkling apple cider instead of Champagne. Try it with fruitier, nonalcoholic ciders, as well as dry-style fermented ciders, to find your perfect fit.

NOTE

- It's very acceptable to make Tinto de Verano with storebought lemon-lime soda instead of the combination of homemade lemon-lime syrup and seltzer. The Spanish soda brand La Casera is popular, and Italian *limonata* works well, too. If using soda, aim for an equal measure to the red wine.

Tinto de Verano
RED WINE & LEMON-LIME SYRUP
TART, JUICY & BUBBLY | HIGHBALL

What's that? You'd like a Radler, but make it wine, you say? I have just the thing. Tinto de Verano is a pairing of red wine and lemon-lime soda. Or, for a fresher take on this classic Spanish refresher, you can whip up some Lemon-Lime Syrup and top the drink with sparkling water, as you see here.

The dark fruit, the acidity, the soft-drink sweetness: what better drink to serve friends as they wash down slices from your new pizza oven, or when you gather round a fire planted in the beach? Tinto de Verano is that simple drink that signals that life is easy, at least for the time one's chilling in your hand.

LEMON-LIME SYRUP

Wash and peel 1 lemon and 1 lime. Add the peels to a pint glass or bowl. Add 1 cup of granulated sugar and gently muddle to release the citrus oils. Add the sugar and muddled peels to a saucepan. Juice and strain lemons and limes (roughly 5 to 6 of each) to yield 8 ounces altogether. Heat until the sugar dissolves. Remove from the heat and leave to cool. Pour into a resealable bottle, straining again to remove solids. Refrigerate for up to 2 to 3 weeks.

SERVES 1

4 ounces red wine, preferably dry, young, and medium-bodied

2 ounces Lemon-Lime Syrup (recipe follows)

GARNISH

Orange wheel (see page 24 to use up your extra citrus)

HAVE HANDY

Cubed ice

Seltzer

Add the wine and syrup to a chilled highball glass and stir briefly to combine. Add ice to fill. Pour seltzer down the neck of the barspoon to top off. Briefly stir once more. Tuck in an orange wheel.

ENHANCEMENTS & DEPARTURES

- Sub 1 ounce of red wine for the same measure of sweet vermouth for a more aromatic Tinto de Verano.

- In a similar spirit to sangria, you can have fun with the fruit garnish here. Blood orange, grapefruit, and lemon are suitable alternatives.

Cuba Libre
RUM & COCA-COLA

CARAMEL, BAKING SPICE & MOLASSES | HIGHBALL

The Cuba Libre is a treasure of Caribbean culture, shared with and beloved by the world. The way the sugarcane undertones of the light rum go hand in hand with the richness, spice, and acidity of Coca-Cola . . . it's a beautiful thing.

This is a drink that is purpose built to enjoy among friends and family. A bottle of rum, a bottle of Coke, a few limes to chop up and squeeze in, and you're on your way to cheersing at any celebration. You can opt to dress down your Cuba Libre in a lowball glass, a red Solo—there are no strict protocols here.

SERVES 1
2 ounces
light rum
4 ounces
Coca-Cola

GARNISH
2 lime wedges
(see page 24 to use up your extra citrus)

HAVE HANDY
Cubed ice

Add the rum to a chilled highball glass. Add ice to nearly fill. Pour the Coca-Cola down the neck of a barspoon. Squeeze 1 lime wedge into the drink and discard. Stir briefly to combine. Hang a lime wedge on the rim of the glass.

Kir Royale
CASSIS & CHAMPAGNE

Creme de cassis is a sweet liqueur made from blackcurrant. It's one-half of the famous sparkling cocktail the Kir Royale. The drink hails from Dijon, France, and is attributed to the city's longtime mayor Félix Kir, who was also a priest and a resistance fighter during World War II. German occupiers stole France's red wine, and so the bubbly Kir Royale and its flat sibling, the Kir, were attempts to reconcoct an approximation for the lost red wine with what was available locally in Dijon.

Europe leads in cassis production, but some American operations are arising, such as New York's C. Cassis, which favors a drier and more botanical expression. (Growing blackcurrants was banned in the US for several decades in the early to mid-1900s because the plant could spread a disease that put pine forests at risk.) In a Kir Royale, the cassis introduces a dark-fruit element to Champagne's bready, stone-fruit profile.

SERVES 1

1 ounce blackcurrant liqueur, such as C. Cassis

4 ounces Champagne, chilled

GARNISH

Lemon twist (see page 24 to use up your extra citrus)

Add the liqueur to a chilled Champagne flute. Gradually pour in the Champagne. Tuck in a lemon twist.

ENHANCEMENTS & DEPARTURES

- While cassis is typically ubiquitous in a Kir Royale, feel free to bend the rules a bit with other berry liqueurs such as Chambord or Crème de mure. If you're feeling extra rebellious, stir up a Kir (sans Royale) and substitute dry white wine for the Champagne.

Tokaji & Bourbon Mist
TOKAJI & BOURBON

HONEY, APRICOT & VANILLA | WINEGLASS

Jane Lopes, the wine expert and former beverage director of Nashville's Catbird Seat, describes this creation of hers as a modified wine. The drink is one of the many wholly original beverages Lopes devised to pair with the cuisine at the renowned Tennessee restaurant when no straight wine would quite match the food perfectly. That said, a Tokaji & Bourbon Mist is superb on its own.

Tokaji comes from a wine region northeast of Budapest, Hungary. The expression we require here is the sweet wine, often served with (or as) dessert. (Dry wines also hail from Tokaji, so be mindful which you're buying.) It's a labor-intensive wine to make, dripping with concentrated fruit flavor and natural sweetness—and it's priced accordingly, so consider enjoying this drink on the most special of occasions.

SERVES 1

5 ounces Tokaji, slightly chilled

Scant ⅛ ounce bourbon

GARNISH

Orange twist
(see page 24 to use up your extra citrus)

If you have an atomizer, spritz an empty wineglass with bourbon until the entire interior surface is coated. Alternatively, you can lightly coat the inside of the glass by adding a small volume of bourbon, about ⅛ ounce, swirling to coat, then pouring out the excess. Add the Tokaji. Garnish with an orange twist.

Champagne Velvet No. 1
CHAMPAGNE & STOUT

VANILLA, COCOA & CREAM | WINEGLASS OR FLUTE

Champagne's bubbles rise. Guinness's bubbles famously fall. Where they intersect is the tasty, sudsy address known as Champagne Velvet No. 1. This drink, sometimes called Black Velvet, deserves that soft, pillowy description because it boasts such a smooth, creamy texture and a mild, inviting flavor. It's a celebration for your palate and therefore welcome at parties everywhere.

SERVES 1

2½ ounces Champagne, chilled

2½ ounces Guinness stout, chilled

Slowly pour the Champagne, then Guinness, into a wineglass or flute—be careful to avoid any overflow. Optionally, the Guinness can be floated on top of the Champagne by pouring it over the back of a wide spoon for a layered look.

Kalimoxto

RED WINE & COCA-COLA

CHERRY, ALLSPICE & BROWN SUGAR | LOWBALL

Fun to say. Fun to drink. Easy to make. That's the Kalimoxto. The pairing of red wine and Coca-Cola, popularized in the Basque region of Spain, may seem like an offense to the wine, but we ought to let go of those perceptions of preciousness. No one mourns the cherry fated for Cherry Coke, so the grapes that give Kalimoxto its fruity overtones should be seen as serving a noble purpose as well.

SERVES 1

2½ ounces red wine, such as Tempranillo, chilled

2½ ounces Coca-Cola

GARNISH

Lemon wheel (optional) (see page 24 to use up your extra citrus)

HAVE HANDY

Cubed ice

Combine the wine and soda in a chilled lowball glass. Gently add ice. Tuck in a lemon wheel, if using.

German Boilermaker
RYE WHISKEY & SCHWARZBIER

CARAMEL, SPICE & TOASTED GRAIN | HIGHBALL

A half liter of inky-black Schwarzbier looks like it's going to put you right to sleep, like chocolate cough syrup. But I find this German beer surprisingly unheavy and refreshing. It has the dark, malty flavors you'd expect, but doesn't conquer your palate the way a stout or porter can. Inspired by the Boilermaker—a mixed drink that's often taken in one swig—this beer highball doubles down on the cereal profile of Schwarzbier with rye whiskey.

This is a version you can sip on. But we aren't going to judge if you wish to make this a true Boilermaker by dropping a shot glass of rye into a pint glass part filled with beer and knocking it back. This is a party cocktail, after all.

SERVES 1

1½ ounces rye whiskey, such as Rittenhouse, chilled

8 ounces Schwarzbier, such as Köstritzer, chilled

Add the whiskey to a chilled highball glass. Gently pour in the Schwarzbier.

Campari Corretto
CAMPARI & SPARKLING WINE

APPLE, GRAPEFRUIT & SOUR CHERRY | FLUTE OR WINEGLASS

This simple drink combining the red bitter liqueur Campari and a fill-up of sparkling wine is reminiscent of both the Spritz (page 152) and the Bellini (page 34) but carries an air of pomp and formality the other two seem to lack. This cocktail would be at home at a dinner party or an upscale cocktail hour. And it's easy enough for guests to mix up themselves.

SERVES 1

1½ ounces Campari

4 ounces sparkling wine, such as prosecco, chilled

GARNISH

Orange twist
(see page 24 to use up your extra citrus)

Add the Campari to a chilled Champagne flute. Gradually pour in the sparkling wine. Tuck in an orange twist.

NOTE

- Your choice of sparkler here could go in a lot of directions, depending on your mood and taste: Spanish cava, Italian Franciacorta, and French crémant d'Alsace will all yield a unique spin on the Corretto.

Picon Bière

AMER PICON & PILSNER

BITTERSWEET ORANGE & CEREAL | HIGHBALL

Anyone who turns down their nose at beer cocktails has clearly never tried a Picon Bière. This French-speaking mixed drink is a café-bar staple combining Amer Picon (look for Bière on the label), the orange-flavored bitter liqueur, and pilsner beer. The two ingredients complement each other magically, so that those under the spell of a Picon Bière have no choice but to gulp it down.

SERVES 1

2 ounces Amer Picon (see Note)

6 ounces European pilsner, such as Radeberger, chilled

GARNISH

Lemon wedge
(see page 24 to use up your extra citrus)

Add the Amer Picon to a chilled highball glass. Pour in the pilsner down the neck of a barspoon. Tuck in a lemon wedge.

NOTE

▪ Because it is currently not imported to the US, Amer Picon can be hard to come by, unless you score a bottle on a trip to France. Other amari are decent substitutes, including Nonino, Ramazzotti, and CioCiara. When substituting, reduce the volume of amaro to 1½ ounces and add ½ ounce of orange liqueur, such as Combier.

Cynanagans Highball
99 BANANAS & CYNAR

BANANAS FOSTER & CINNAMON | HIGHBALL

This recipe by the inventive New York–based bartender Kitty Bernardo is perfectly at home at a house party, a tiki night, and anywhere else banana fans (banatics?) hang out. Bernardo developed this highball based on an unlikely ingredient pairing suggested to her by a bartender friend, Chris Elford. She was skeptical until she tried it.

The 99 Bananas—a banana liqueur and dorm-room fixture so named because it's 99 proof—is wildly strong and powerfully sweet alone but is tame and dessert-like when balanced with an equal measure of the artichoke-based bitter liqueur Cynar.

SERVES 1
½ ounce
99 Bananas
½ ounce Cynar

GARNISH
Lime twist
Orange twist
(see page 24 to use up your extra citrus)

HAVE HANDY
Ice cubes
Seltzer
Angostura bitters

Add the 99 Bananas and Cynar to a chilled highball glass. Add 1 dash Angostura bitters and ice cubes to fill. Stir for five revolutions to chill the ingredients slightly then top off with seltzer, about 4 ounces. Stir slowly for two revolutions and tamp down the ice once to fully incorporate the seltzer. Express lime and orange twists and add them to the glass.

Smoky Paloma Radler
MEZCAL & CITRUS ALE

SMOKE, GRAPEFRUIT & HOPS | HIGHBALL

What if a Paloma and a Radler had a love child? Meet that drink. Isn't it darling? The former is a combination of agave spirit and grapefruit juice, and the latter is a beer cocktail that typically pairs light- and medium-bodied beers with citrus juice, often lemonade. The center of their Venn diagram is a combination of smoky, savory mezcal and citrus ale.

The Dogfish Head bottling recommended here is practically a Radler on its own—juicy with lots of grapefruit-peel zing, making it a believable stand-in for citrus. This is a drink that backyard barbecues didn't know they needed.

SERVES 1

1½ ounces
mezcal

6 ounces citrus
ale, preferably
Dogfish Head
Citrus Squall,
chilled

GARNISH

2 lime wedges
(see page 24 to use up
your extra citrus)

Add the mezcal to a chilled highball glass. Gently pour in the citrus ale. Squeeze 1 lime wedge into the drink and discard. Stir briefly to combine. Hang a lime wedge on the rim of the glass.

ENHANCEMENTS & DEPARTURES

- For a little extra zing, salt the rim of your highball glass: run one of the lime wedges along the rim of the glass, holding it upside down so the juice doesn't run down the glass. While the rim is still wet, dip the rim into a salt-filled saucer. Alternatively, you can sprinkle salt onto the glass.

SLOW

Albert Einstein wrote of time that "the distinction between the past, present and future is only a stubbornly persistent illusion." While we turn over the big thoughts in life, might I suggest you put one of the following cocktails in your hand. Feel the weight of it. Or, as Einstein probably would have put, feel the way in which its mass curves space. These are drinks you can fall into. They enable you—in a self-deceptive way, at least—to experience time slowing down. That is, if we agree time even exists.

What makes a Slow Jam? Primarily, a greater heft of spirit than many of the drinks you'll find throughout this book. In fact, they combine two liquors together, as opposed to, say, a spirit and a nonalcoholic mixer. Their flavors are bolder and darker. Think bitter, woodsy, toasted, nutty. To make them, you'll typically need your mixing glass

JAMS

and barspoon so the ingredients can be stirred over ice. And, as the name suggests, you're likely going to enjoy these drinks over more minutes than something like a highball, despite their being smaller in volume. You sip a Slow Jam.

You'll find here a host of Scotch-based drinks, like the Rusty Nail and the Godfather, which relish in the malty, smoky, oaky qualities of this beloved style of whisky. Many classic gin cocktails are collected here, as well, including a personal favorite, the Dry Martini, and its pickled counterpart, the Gibson. For those who enjoy a Manhattan, take the Moto Guzzi for a test drive. And for the bitter-brave, skip to . . . Don't Judge, a cocktail that's as irrational as the paradox of quantum superposition—and yet there it is, tasting pretty damn good.

Dry Martini (& Gibson)

GIN & VERMOUTH

JUNIPER, FLORA, CITRUS & BRINE | COUPE OR NICK & NORA

The Dry Martini and Gibson are forever kinds of drinks. They'll never fall out of favor. When you can't decide on what drink you want, resort to one of these and you'll wind up pleased.

I've paired them up here because they are prepared very similarly and only diverge at the garnishing stage. These classics pedestal the clean and mutually botanical qualities of their paired ingredients, gin and dry vermouth, but juxtapose those flavors differently based on the garnish.

To go bright and shiny with your Dry Martini, finish with a lemon coin. For a slightly more savory version of the drink, instead use the most delicious green olive you can find. The Gibson starts with the same liquid prep. The final flourish is to use a Cocktail Onion. If you're not familiar, a Cocktail Onion is a pearl onion—an onion of diminutive size, about the size of a large olive—that's been peeled and pickled in herbs and spices.

SERVES 1

2 ounces London dry gin, such as Martin Miller's or Broker's

1 ounce dry vermouth, such as Dolin Dry or Noilly Prat Extra Dry

GARNISH

Dry Martini:
Green olive
(such as Castelvetrano)
or lemon coin

Cocktail Onion
(recipe follows)

HAVE HANDY

Cubed ice

Add the gin and vermouth to a mixing glass. Add ice and stir for 30 seconds. Strain into a chilled coupe or Nick & Nora glass. For a Dry Martini, drop in a skewered green olive, or express and drop in a lemon coin (i.e., a quarter-size disc of lemon peel, cut from the widest part of the fruit, with minimal pith). Garnish a Gibson with a skewered Cocktail Onion.

ENHANCEMENTS & DEPARTURES

- A couple of dashes of orange bitters in a Dry Martini—added to the mixing glass pre-ice—takes this drink from delicious to sublime.

COCKTAIL ONIONS

To give your Gibson a personal, handcrafted touch, make your own Cocktail Onions. Carefully peel 6 to 10 pearl onions and add them to a sterilized mason jar. Create a pickling brine: bring to a simmer 1 cup water, ⅓ cup granulated sugar, 1⅓ cups vinegar of your choice (white, balsamic, sherry, or combinations thereof), and 2 tablespoons salt along with your choice of herbs and spices (e.g., black peppercorns, bay leaves, coriander pods, cloves, thyme, fennel seed, chili flakes). Let the brine cool, then pour over the onions, seal, and gently agitate to distribute the contents. Refrigerate overnight before enjoying, and store in the fridge for up to 2 weeks.

Rusty Nail
SCOTCH & DRAMBUIE

The Rusty Nail is what an Old-Fashioned would be if it visited Scotland and decided to never leave. It combines blended Scotch whisky and the Scotch-based sweet liqueur Drambuie. Scotch gets a lot of its flavor profile from malted barley, which lends the spirit a sweet-cereal backbone, counterbalancing the brooding, peated smokiness. Drambuie is like Scotch's more outgoing friend, full of honey and spice notes. When two ingredients go so well with each other, it's no wonder this old drink has stuck around.

SERVES 1

2 ounces blended Scotch whisky, such as Johnny Walker Black Label

1 ounce Drambuie

GARNISH

Lemon twist
(see page 24 to use up your extra citrus)

HAVE HANDY

Cubed ice

Large ice cube
(optional)

Add the Scotch and Drambuie to a mixing glass. Add cubed ice and stir for 30 seconds. Strain into a lowball glass filled with cubed ice, or a large ice cube. Express and drop in a lemon twist.

Dubonnet Cocktail
DUBONNET ROUGE & GIN

NUTTY, BITTERSWEET & HERBACEOUS | COUPE OR NICK & NORA

Dubonnet Rouge is a sweet-leaning aperitif from France that contains quinine, the same bitter ingredient that flavors tonic water. It's richer than sweet vermouth and assumes a big presence in the drinks it shows up in. (No surprise, then, that it gets sole billing in the title of this drink.) Supposedly Queen Elizabeth II would regularly treat herself to Dubonnet Cocktails. If it's good enough for the queen, who lived to be ninety-six, it's certainly good enough for us.

SERVES 1

¾ ounce
Dubonnet Rouge

1½ ounces
London dry gin

GARNISH

Lemon twist
(see page 24 to use up your extra citrus)

HAVE HANDY

Cubed ice

Add the Dubonnet Rouge and gin to a mixing glass. Add ice and stir for 30 seconds. Strain into a chilled coupe or Nick & Nora glass. Express and drop in a lemon twist.

Godfather
SCOTCH & AMARETTO

MARZIPAN, SMOKE & SWEET ORANGE | LOWBALL

I think amaretto gets a bad rap. Some of the mass-market bottlings have become too sweet to be enjoyable, and that holds back this centuries-old almond-flavored liqueur from getting more use in drinkers' home bars. Moreover, many amaretto cocktails aren't that good even on their best days. But the Godfather is an exception.

Seek out an amaretto that has remained true to the traditional tenets of the category (I like Caffo, but there are other tasty, noncloying expressions), and be sure to lay down a healthy spray of an orange twist to draw out similar flavors in the amaretto.

SERVES 1

2 ounces blended Scotch whisky, such as Johnny Walker Black Label

¾ ounce amaretto, preferably Caffo

GARNISH

Orange twist
(see page 24 to use up your extra citrus)

HAVE HANDY

Cubed ice

Large ice cube
(optional)

Add the Scotch and amaretto to a mixing glass. Add cubed ice and stir for 30 seconds. Strain into a lowball glass filled with cubed ice, or a large ice cube. Express and drop in an orange twist.

M&M

MEZCAL & ITALIAN AMARO

This duo of mezcal and amaro joins together two of the darlings of the modern cocktail establishment. You have the fragrant, smoky Mexican-made agave spirit and the bitter liqueur synonymous with Italy. It's kismet that they go well together.

This drink is popularly known as the M&M because Montenegro, an amaro from Bologna, works particularly well in this 1:1 template. But, thanks to the contemporary proliferation of both categories of spirit, you can recast this cocktail dozens of times, trying out different marriages to find your ideal match.

SERVES 1

1½ ounces mezcal, such as Del Maguey Vida

1½ ounces amaro, preferably Montenegro

GARNISH

Orange twist
(see page 24 to use up your extra citrus)

HAVE HANDY

Cubed ice

Large ice cube
(optional)

Add the mezcal and amaro to a mixing glass. Add cubed ice and stir for 30 seconds. Strain into a lowball glass filled with cubed ice, or a large ice cube. Express and drop in an orange twist.

Alaska

YELLOW CHARTREUSE & GIN

FRESH HERBS, HONEY & GREEN VEGETABLES |
COUPE OR NICK & NORA

The Alaska cocktail is strong but tender. The drink is at least 100 years old, arising around the time when bartenders were stirring up offshoots of the Dry Martini. Here, instead of the gin being modified by dry vermouth, as in the Dry Martini, we use the French monk-made herbal liqueur called Yellow Chartreuse, a dynamo of botanical flavors that makes gin seem tame in comparison. Mix an Alaska when you're in for one cocktail and wish to treat your palate to a single act of theatrics.

SERVES 1

½ ounce Yellow Chartreuse

1½ ounces London dry gin, such as Tanqueray

HAVE HANDY

Cubed ice

Add the Yellow Chartreuse and gin to a mixing glass. Add ice and stir for 30 seconds. Strain into a chilled coupe or Nick & Nora glass.

ENHANCEMENTS & DEPARTURES

▪ Similar to a Dry Martini (page 118), the Alaska can be made more complex with 2 dashes of orange bitters.

Hall & Oates

COFFEE LIQUEUR & FERNET-BRANCA

What collection of boozy stirred cocktails would be complete without one that's so broodingly dark, it's like staring into a cave in the middle of the night?

This build of coffee liqueur and the burly, balsam-flavored amaro Fernet-Branca is courtesy of St. George Spirits. It's invigorating and luscious, with just enough sweetness to balance out the intense flavors of the amaro and coffee liqueur.

SERVES 1

1½ ounces coffee liqueur, such as St. George NOLA

1½ ounces Fernet-Branca

HAVE HANDY

Cubed ice

Add the coffee liqueur and Fernet-Branca to a mixing glass. Add ice and stir for 30 seconds. Strain into a chilled coupe or Nick & Nora glass.

Debonair

SCOTCH & GINGER LIQUEUR

This is a modern classic created by the prolific cocktail historian and drink maker Gary Regan in the 1990s. The pairing of Scotch and ginger liqueur is a heavenly match. The warming, sharp spice of ginger is soprano to the Scotch's sultry, smoky baritone. Blended Scotches will work for this cocktail, but the preferred move is to enjoy it with a single malt. It's not for every mixed drink calling for Scotch that you'd spill such precious juice, but your Debonair will be better for it.

SERVES 1

2½ ounces Scotch whisky, preferably single malt

1 ounce ginger liqueur, such as Domaine de Canton

GARNISH

Lemon twist
(see page 24 to use up your extra citrus)

HAVE HANDY

Cubed ice

Add the Scotch and ginger liqueur to a mixing glass. Add ice and stir for 30 seconds. Strain into a chilled coupe or Nick & Nora glass. Express and drop in a lemon twist.

133

Ferrari

CAMPARI & FERNET-BRANCA

MINTY, UNCTUOUS & CITRUS PITH **|** LOWBALL

As bracing as a lap in an F1 racer, this drink is known for being a so-called bartenders' handshake—a challenging but delicious cocktail for those whose palates like (or have been trained to like) muscularly bitter flavors. It can be slugged as a shot (see instructions below) or sipped from an ice-cold lowball glass. Personally, I think it's worth savoring a Ferrari over time rather than sprinting to the finish line, but I'll leave that up to you.

SERVES 1

1½ ounces Campari

1½ ounces Fernet-Branca

HAVE HANDY

Cubed ice

Add the Campari and Fernet-Branca to a mixing glass. Add ice and stir for 30 seconds. Strain into a frozen lowball glass filled with cubed ice.

ENHANCEMENTS & DEPARTURES

- To prepare a round of undiluted, shot-format versions of this drink, combine equal measures of Campari and Fernet-Branca in a bottle (3 ounces of each will yield 4 servings), and chill in the freezer for at least 30 minutes. Pour 1½ ounces per shot.

Moto Guzzi

BOURBON & PUNT E MES

Think of this cocktail as a shortcut to a Manhattan. Whereas that drink—a cocktail in the historical sense of the word—combines whiskey, sweet vermouth, and bitters, the Moto Guzzi leans on Punt e Mes, an Italian vermouth that's "half bitter" (hence "e Mes"), to do the work of the vermouth and the bitters, all in one dosage. Efficiency without sacrificing flavor or depth. I love the viscosity of this drink; it embraces the palate as a big-shouldered cocktail should.

SERVES 1

1¾ ounces overproof bourbon, such as Wild Turkey 101

1¼ ounces Punt e Mes

HAVE HANDY

Cubed ice

Large ice cube (optional)

Add the bourbon and Punt e Mes to a mixing glass. Add cubed ice and stir for 30 seconds. Strain into a lowball glass filled with cubed ice, or a large ice cube.

ENHANCEMENTS & DEPARTURES

- The original specs of this drink (developed by bartender John Gertsen) call for Booker's Bourbon, which is bottled without any dilution, usually around 120 proof. If you opt to use it—be warned, bottles of Booker's, like well-aged bourbons in general, have gotten quite expensive (but are well worth the investment)—adjust the measurements to 1½ ounces for both ingredients.

...Don't Judge

ANGOSTURA BITTERS & JÄGERMEISTER

BARK, BITE & BITTER LEMON | LOWBALL

This little drink punches above its weight class. Bartender Toby Maloney concocted this recipe, whose full name is, ahem, "Shut the fuck up, drink it and don't judge." (The titling is his; the paraphrasing is mine.) Jägermeister is probably the most misunderstood spirit, in that it's primarily treated like it's radioactive and must be dispensed with immediately (usually as a shot).

But when one takes a moment to really taste Jäger, to attempt to appreciate it, its true nature as a complex German amaro starts to emerge. This drink, which augments ice-cold Jäger with a few shakes of bitters and a dousing of expressed lemon oil, is the epitome of a Slow Jam. Drink it in, and enjoy it more than you ever expected to.

SERVES 1

3 dashes Angostura bitters

2 ounces Jägermeister, freezer-chilled

GARNISH

2 lemon twists, oversized (see page 24 to use up your extra citrus)

Add the bitters to a chilled lowball glass. Pour in the ice-cold Jägermeister. Cut a large swath of lemon peel and express the oils over the glass. Discard the peel and tuck in a generous lemon twist.

SOME A
REQ

An argument running through this book is that the degree of difficulty in making a cocktail needn't be a prerequisite for goodness. Said differently, a simply made drink can be as great as its more complicated peers, so long as the ingredients are well chosen, the proportions are dialed in, and the technique involved—albeit approachable—is carried out with care. We've looked to and celebrated the sort of pour that results in outsize satisfaction relative to the elementary effort invested. Cold fusion in a jar . . . strained into a cocktail glass.

But as you get more proficient at making drinks, and the bottles you collect at home become more plentiful—and I hope working through the recipes in this book spurs both—there's going to be an urge to do more, to continue to push out your boundaries as a home bartender. That has been my experience as I have gone deeper into this pursuit. One new frontier to explore, brought forth by the drinks in this section, is making some ingredients from scratch. We've already done this, maybe without noticing, when we embarked on the Cocktail Onions that garnish a Gibson, the Clarified Lime Juice that perks up a Gin Rickey, and the Cream of Coconut that sweetens an Absinthe Coconut Frappé. The cocktail you make at home is inherently homemade, but there's something extra special—and especially rewarding—about a cocktail that includes an ingredient you make yourself.

SEMBLY
IRED

For each two-ingredient cocktail that follows, there is a recipe-within-a-recipe, enabling you to lend your homemade drinks more of what in Korea they call *son-mat*, or what in Mexico is known as *sazón*. The approximation in English is "hand taste"—the unique influence of the hands of the cook. As it happens, those countries' cuisines will also serve as our inspiration. For a delightful nonalcoholic spritz, we'll brew up a Pine Needle Syrup, and to make a fruity, coffee-laced highball, we'll first cook up a batch of sour-spicy-sweet Chamoy. We'll also get better acquainted with orgeat, shrub, and cordial, three versatile types of cocktail modifiers. If none of these things are at all familiar to you, that's a good thing.

As a practical matter, these drinks require you to do some work in advance. (Look elsewhere in this book if what you need is a drink, *à la minute*.) The subrecipes are not challenging; they just take a little extra time. They suit occasions where you may wish to flex your culinary muscle, like throwing a dinner party. Or maybe you're attending a friend's gathering and you say, "What can I bring?" and they say, "Just bring yourself!" Now you've got a variety of ways to do that, while also not showing up empty-handed.

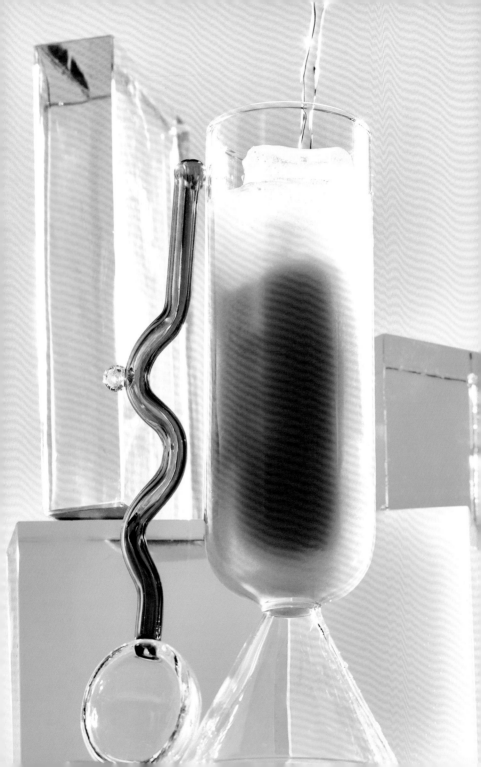

Mauresque
PASTIS & ORGEAT

Pastis is a star anise–flavored liqueur synonymous with the French port city of Marseille. It's a staple of French drinking culture, often served alongside chilled water and/or ice, allowing the drinker to dilute the robust liqueur to their taste. Like its cousin, absinthe, pastis contains heavy doses of botanical oils that are held in solution by the spirit's high alcohol content. Once it's diluted, pastis fogs up to a milky pastel yellow due to the precipitation of the oils.

The Mauresque (sometimes called Momisette) pairs pastis with another French creation, orgeat—a concentrated, aromatic almond syrup. Sipping on this drink, you can practically feel the cooling sea breeze along the Côte d'Azur. You can purchase shelf-stable orgeat, but making your own can yield a much fuller-flavored product. It's somewhat of a project but doesn't involve any complicated culinary techniques.

SERVES 1

2 ounces pastis, such as Ricard
1 ounce Orgeat (recipe follows)

HAVE HANDY

Cubed ice (optional)
Seltzer, chilled

Add the pastis and Orgeat to a chilled highball glass. Gently stir to combine. Add ice, if using. Pour seltzer down the neck of a barspoon to top.

ORGEAT

Toast ¾ cup of raw, skin-on almonds in a pan until fragrant. Place in a resealable container with 1 cup of water. Soak at room temperature overnight. Strain, reserving the liquid. Top off the liquid with water to reach 1½ cups. Recombine the almonds and liquid and blend well. Strain through a cheesecloth. Add ¾ cup each of granulated and packed brown sugars, transfer to a saucepan, and gently heat just enough for the sugars to dissolve. Let cool and add 1 barspoon each of orange flower and rose water, and ½ ounce of brandy. Transfer to a resealable bottle and store in the refrigerator for up to 1 month. Separation is normal; just agitate periodically.

Garibaldi

CAMPARI & CITRUS JUICE

SWEET ORANGE, GRAPEFRUIT PEEL & CHERRY | HIGHBALL

The Garibaldi is living its best life. It's just the right amount of bitter to be assertive, just the right amount of sweet to be genteel. It feels special, but casual. It's exciting on the palate yet a study in simplicity. The Garibaldi works as a brunch cocktail but can just as easily dress up an evening. And when you make the blend of freshly squeezed citrus juices for this cocktail, you could even convince yourself that this drink is good for you. (At the very least, your soul.)

The cocktail is named after Giuseppe Garibaldi, the general who was instrumental in bringing the north and south of Italy together as one unified nation. In some ways, Garibaldi the drink salutes unity, too. It marries Campari, hailing from Milan in the north, with citrus fruits, which are prevalent in the Italian south.

SERVES 1

1¾ ounces Campari

4½ ounces Citrus Juice Blend
(pre-blended volume; recipe follows)

GARNISH

Grapefruit slice
(see page 24 to use up your extra citrus)

HAVE HANDY

Cubed ice

SPECIAL TOOL

Immersion blender (see Note)

Prepare the Citrus Juice Blend 30 minutes prior to serving. Add ice to a chilled highball glass. Add the Campari and Citrus Juice Blend. Briefly stir. Tuck in a grapefruit slice.

CITRUS JUICE BLEND

Juice 1 grapefruit, 1 orange (or blood orange, if available), and 1 lemon, and mix their juices in a 1:1¼ ratio, respectively. (One of each fruit should yield enough juice for one cocktail.) Strain through a sieve, removing any large pulp or seed parts. Refrigerate for at least 30 minutes. Once chilled, measure out 4½ ounces and add to a pint glass or shaker tin. Submerge the business end of an immersion blender and froth with brief pulses. Use immediately.

NOTE

In a pinch, you can make a good
Garibaldi with Campari and freshly
squeezed orange juice using the same
booze-to-juice proportions as noted
in the recipe. If you don't have an
immersion blender, a conventional
blender will also do the trick. As a
last resort, shake the juice with a
cube of ice in a cocktail shaker.

NOTE

- The Strawberry Shrub Syrup recipe can serve as a template for a variety of shrubs. Substitute other berries, stone fruit, or combinations of them, to your liking. Try them with other unaged spirits, such as vodka, gin, mezcal, and light rum.

Sour Strawberry Highball

TEQUILA & STRAWBERRY SHRUB SYRUP

TINGLY, RIPE & REFRESHING | HIGHBALL

Scenario: you loaded up on fruit, and it's ripening faster than you can eat it. You're worried it's descending into mushiness (or, worse, fuzziness). It's time to get shrubbing—a lifeline for at-risk fruit. Shrub refers to a centuries-old beverage designed for preservation composed of ripened fruit, sugar, and vinegar. Shrubs are typically heady, funky, lip-smackingly tart concoctions. Think of it as a snapshot of fruit at peak tastiness. Shrub is a bit too pungent to drink on its own, but as a cocktail ingredient, this boldly flavorful brew is fantastic.

The model of spirit plus shrub, topped off with seltzer, as used in this tequila-based highball recipe, is highly modifiable. I like the pairing of vegetal agave spirit with the concentrated, candy-like flavor of macerated strawberry. But when you go shrubbing, you're welcome to mingle with other spirits and other fruits.

SERVES 1

2 ounces tequila

1 ounce **Strawberry Shrub Syrup** (recipe follows)

GARNISH

Lime wheel (see page 24 to use up your extra citrus)

HAVE HANDY

Cubed ice

Seltzer

Add the tequila and Strawberry Shrub Syrup to a chilled highball glass. Briefly stir to mix. Nearly fill with ice. Pour seltzer down the neck of a barspoon to top. Garnish with a lime wheel.

STRAWBERRY SHRUB SYRUP

Wash, trim, and quarter 1 pound of ripe strawberries. Add to a mixing bowl with 2 cups of granulated sugar and toss to coat. Gently mash the fruit with a fork. Cover and let stand at room temperature for 1 hour, then refrigerate for at least 1 day (but 2 is ideal), periodically shaking the container to redistribute the contents. Mix in 1½ cups of apple cider vinegar, then strain and transfer the mixture into a resealable bottle, squeezing out as much liquid as you can. Refrigerate and use within 2 weeks.

Whiskey Sour

BOURBON & LEMON CORDIAL

TANNINS, VANILLA & LEMON PIE | COUPE

Sours hide in plain sight across the cocktail map. This classification of drink covers mixtures consisting of a spirit, an acidic element—usually citrus juice—and a sweet element such as simple syrup or sweet liqueur. Classic cocktails such as the Gimlet, Margarita, and Daiquiri are all examples. The proven playbook of boozy-plus-sour-plus-sweet-equals-balance allows bartenders to mix and match components and make practically endless iterations on the Sour.

A Whiskey Sour is a great drink on its own but can also be your springboard into Sour experimentation. The deeper, barrel-aged notes of a good bourbon and the bright, high notes of lemon nicely complement each other. By pairing the bourbon with Lemon Cordial you made ahead of time, this Whiskey Sour comes together faster and easier (cordial is like two ingredients in one), and it shows off a "juicier," more dynamic expression of lemon flavor. Once you have a batch of Lemon Cordial handy, you can test it out with other spirits, like gin and vodka, and mess with modifiers that add bitterness, fruitiness, herbal aromas, and more. So go forth and find your signature Sour.

SERVES 1

2 ounces bourbon

¾ ounce Lemon Cordial
(recipe follows)

GARNISH

Brandied cherry

HAVE HANDY

Cubed ice

Add the bourbon and Lemon Cordial to a shaker. Add ice and shake for 10 seconds. Double strain into a chilled coupe glass. Straddle a skewered brandied cherry across the rim of the glass.

LEMON CORDIAL

Clean, thoroughly dry, and peel 5 lemons. Set aside the peels, then juice the lemons. Strain off the pulp. Combine the juice and ¾ cup of granulated sugar in a saucepan and warm over low heat. Remove from the heat before the mixture reaches a boil. Let cool, then add in the lemon peels. Transfer the contents to a resealable container and refrigerate overnight. Strain the cordial into a resealable container. Keep refrigerated; use within 2 weeks.

NOTE

- Drinkers' tolerance for acid varies. If you find this ratio of 2 parts bourbon to ¾ part cordial is too spirit forward for you, increase the amount of cordial in ¼-ounce increments to your preference.

ENHANCEMENTS & DEPARTURES

- The texture and acidity level of a Sour is often improved by the addition of egg whites, which, when shaken, create a fluffy foam. Add one egg white to the shaker alongside the bourbon and Lemon Cordial. Vigorously shake the liquids without ice inside (known as a dry shake) for 30 seconds. Add ice, shake again for 10 seconds, then strain. Lay down a few drops of Angostura bitters atop the foam top for aroma.

Chamoy & Coffee Highball

COFFEE LIQUEUR & CHAMOY SYRUP

RED WINE, CHOCOLATE & HIBISCUS | HIGHBALL

The Brooklyn bartender Kat Foster turned me on to Chamoy, a fixture of Mexican kitchens, and its potential as a cocktail ingredient. Commonly rendered as a sauce, Chamoy is spicy, sweet, salty, and sour, all at once. Its magic comes from the intermingling of hibiscus flowers, dried fruit (usually prune and apricot), and chiles. The stuff can also be prepared as a syrup, like the version here, which is based on Foster's method of preparation.

This highball, which has Chamoy playing opposite coffee liqueur, is the bottomless color of Homer's wine-dark seas and—perhaps for that reason—reminds me of drinking Lambrusco, the sweet Italian sparkling wine. There's so much going on in the glass here, yet each flavor in the ensemble resonates deeply.

SERVES 1

1½ ounces coffee liqueur, such as Mr. Black

1½ ounces Chamoy Syrup (recipe follows)

HAVE HANDY

Cubed ice

Seltzer

Add the coffee liqueur and Chamoy Syrup to a chilled highball glass. Nearly fill with ice. Pour seltzer down the neck of a barspoon to top. Briefly stir to mix.

CHAMOY SYRUP

Toast 2 dried ancho chiles in a saucepan. Add, by weight, 1 ounce dried hibiscus flowers; 2 ounces dried apricots, halved; 3½ ounces dried prunes, halved; and 10 ounces granulated sugar. Add, by volume, 10 ounces water and 1 teaspoon salt. Bring to a boil, then quickly reduce the heat to low and simmer for 10 minutes. Remove from the heat and add in a fresh jalapeño, sliced. Cover the saucepan and let cool for at least 20 minutes, then transfer to a resealable glass bottle while straining out the solids. Keep refrigerated for up to 3 weeks.

Pine Sudachi Spritz
PINE NEEDLE SYRUP & SUDACHI

This recipe is courtesy of Han Suk Cho, a California-based bartender who specializes in zero-proof cocktails. Many of her creations derive from memories of her upbringing in Korea; here she was inspired by *sol ip-chung*, a syrup made by packing young pine needles in sugar, which her grandmother would make. Over months, the sugar slowly draws out the moisture and flavor contained in the needles.

The Pine Needle Syrup here won't take you months to make; it uses pine needle tea and fresh mint to capture the invigorating forest aroma that makes this spirit-free cocktail special. The herbal-and-citrus flavor profile adds up to be much like gin, making this drink an alcohol-free alternative to a classic Gin & Tonic.

SERVES 1

1 ounce Pine Needle Syrup
(recipe follows)

¾ ounce sudachi (or yuzu) juice

HAVE HANDY

Cubed ice

Seltzer

In a chilled highball glass, combine the Pine Needle Syrup and sudachi juice. Add ice and briefly stir. Pour seltzer down the neck of a barspoon to top.

PINE NEEDLE SYRUP

Prepare a simple syrup with 5 ounces each of water and granulated sugar by heating them together in a small saucepan. Once the sugar is fully dissolved, remove the pan from heat. Add 3 ounces of pine needle tea and a handful of mint sprigs. Transfer to a resealable container and allow to steep overnight. Transfer to a resealable container while straining out the solids. Keep refrigerated; use within 2 weeks.

Brandy Flip

SWEET EGG & BRANDY DE JEREZ

It's hard to pin down the Flip. To eighteenth-century drinkers in England, a Flip combined rum, brandy, ale, and sugar that was goosed by a red-hot poker. The sudden thrust of high heat bubbled and caramelized the sugars, creating a frothy, inebriating confection. (I picture a blacksmith moonlighting as a tavernkeeper behind this.) The designation took on new meaning in America as the country's cocktail culture established itself in the nineteenth century. Egg became a key ingredient, while ale became less common; beating the egg into a lather would serve as a proxy for the stab of hot iron. Much like Sours, you can make a Flip using a variety of base spirits.

The Brandy Flip emerges out of the American Flip tradition as a mix of brandy, egg, and simple syrup, dusted with nutmeg. It doesn't get much attention, and I think that's a shame. It brings out the best qualities of brandy, including notes of dried fruit and baking spice. Its pillowy texture is so satisfying. Typically, the egg and spirit would be mixed in a shaker tin with simple syrup, but since egg already has a large percentage of water, I employ a slightly different technique here.

SERVES 1

2 ounces Sweet Egg (recipe follows)

2 ounces Brandy de Jerez, such as Lustau or Cardinal Mendoza

GARNISH

Ground nutmeg

HAVE HANDY

Cubed ice

Prepare the Sweet Egg. Add 2 ounces to a shaker along with the brandy. Dry shake (with no ice) for 20 seconds. Open the shaker and add cubed ice. Shake again for another 10 seconds. Double strain the contents into a chilled coupe glass. Dust the surface with a pinch of ground nutmeg.

SWEET EGG

Combine in a mixing bowl superfine sugar and whole eggs in a ratio of 1 ounce of sugar for every 1 egg. (A mixture using 1 egg will yield roughly 2 ounces of Sweet Egg, or enough to make 1 Brandy Flip.) Whisk vigorously for about 1 minute, until the beaten mixture appears frothy, and you can no longer detect any undissolved sugar. If preparing in advance (no more than 30 minutes before serving, or the mixture will get clumpy), whisk again immediately prior to use.

ACKNOWLEDGMENTS

I doubt I'll ever feel I was worthy of being given these pages to fill. My view of the world of cocktails has been that of the amateur, the journalist—gazing in from the outside; wielding only a home office from which to hone my craft. I asked myself, *Who am I to program radio stations on someone else's car?* All I hope is that I've done justice to an institution I admire and respect so much.

Cut to my gushing gratitude for Darian Keels of Clarkson Potter, whose title as editor of this book speaks to only a fraction of her talents and contributions. Thank you, Darian, for your coaching, your creativity, and the calm you gifted me at all the right moments. The confidence to believe I could do this came from you.

I'm so grateful to all the people at Clarkson Potter who cared for this book over many months. Thank you to Jennifer Sit for taking a chance on a first-time author and for nurturing this idea. I'm indebted to Stephanie Huntwork and her gorgeously polished art direction and design. Liana Faughnan and Anne Cherry, thank you for each of the countless enhancements you made to the text.

To the team who came together to produce the photography for the book, I'm amazed by your magic. Thank you to photographers Chris Sue-Chu and Alyssa Wodabek, along with food stylist Melanie Stuparyk and prop stylist Andrea McCrindle. I want to go live in the world you conjured up for these drinks.

Talia Baiocchi of PUNCH has long been a guiding light for me in my cocktail writing, and she has graciously helped shine the way toward this project. Thank you, Talia, for being a champion in so many ways.

I owe my education in drinks to dozens of bartenders, especially those who make Chicago's bars a beacon of warmth and hospitality. One of my first and most formative cocktail classes was taught by Paul McGee, then at the Whistler; Paul, your knowledge and curiosity have been an inspiration. You and others welcomed me into your bars, and community, with open arms.

Anthony Todd provided friendly enablement, and an outlet at The Chicagoist, for me to geek out on cocktails while finding my footing as a drinks writer. I am perennially grateful to Maggie Hoffman for always being ready with the right suggestion or insight to make my reporting and recipes better. And Faith Durand and the team at The Kitchn gave me the impetus to study the classic cocktail canon through a weekly column called 9-Bottle Bar.

I'm thankful to the many bartenders and industry professionals who graciously lent their time and creativity through the recipe contributions they made here. Kitty Bernardo, Han Suk Cho, Jane Lopes, Sother Teague, and Toby Maloney: I'm such a fan of your work! Kat Foster sent me down such exciting and unfamiliar paths. And Ellie Winters, you and the St. George family are class acts.

I want to thank my family—wife, Karen, and kids, Zadie and Kai—for being there for me, always. Karen, you were not only an invaluable sounding board (and taster) throughout this process but also granted me the time and space to spin yet another plate while so many others were already going.

Last but foremost, I thank my father, Stephan Kamholz, to whom this book is dedicated. My dad was a true renaissance man, whose infectious enthusiasm and boundless knowledge for beverages brought joy to the lives of so many loved ones and friends. I feel so fortunate I had your footsteps to follow, and for all the drinks we shared.

INDEX